TODD ENGLISH'S

RUSTIC PIZZA

HANDMADE ARTISAN PIES FROM YOUR OWN KITCHEN

TODD ENGLISH & HEATHER RODINO

CASTLE POINT BOOKS
NEW YORK

Todd English's Rustic Pizza copyright © 2017 by St. Martin's Press.
All rights reserved.
Printed in the United States of America. For information,
address St. Martin's Press, 175 Fifth Avenue, New York, N.Y. 10010.

www.castlepointbooks.com
www.stmartins.com

The Castle Point Books trademark is owned by Castle Point Publications, LLC.
Castle Point books are published and distributed by St. Martin's Press.

ISBN 978-1-250-14767-7 (paper over board)

Photography by Allan Penn

Design by Katie Jennings Campbell

Production by Mary Velgos

Our books may be purchased in bulk for promotional, educational, or business use. Please
contact your local bookseller or the Macmillan Corporate and Premium Sales Department at
1-800-221-7945, extension 5442, or by e-mail at MacmillanSpecialMarkets@macmillan.com.

First Edition: November 2017
10 9 8 7 6 5 4 3 2 1

CONTENTS

4 VEGGIE PIZZAS 65

5 MEAT PIZZAS 123

6 SEAFOOD PIZZAS 181

7 SICILIAN-STYLE PIZZAS 193

INTRODUCTION

For many years, my motto has been "Never trust a round pizza." An artisanal rustic pizza, made lovingly by hand, will never be perfectly round like its mass-produced counterpart. That imperfection—the fact that it's a little different every time—is what makes rustic pizza special. And I should know. I've been obsessed with pizza for a long time. Ever since I lived and worked in Italy, I ate every kind of pizza I could lay my hands on. I went north, south, east, and west—all over the country, trying all of the amazing pizzas I could find. From its origins in Naples to newer international influences, pizza is endlessly adaptable and never gets boring. With all of the varied and innovative recipes in this book, I promise that you will never look at pizza the same way again.

One of the most fascinating things I learned from my long research into all things pizza is that this food we now call pizza is actually a recent iteration of an ancient style of food, based on enhancing the nutritional and flavor profiles of bread. Since ancient times, people have been adding various toppings to bread, and cultures around the world have their own flatbreads. In fact, pizza is thought to have evolved from an Egyptian flatbread. But there's also naan from Central and South Asia, pita from the Middle East, injera from Ethopia, lavash from Armenia, flatbrød from Norway, tortillas from Mexico, and dozens of other flatbreads from all over the world. Many of these are served with traditional toppings, stuffed, or torn and used to scoop up foods. Like these other foods, pizza is essentially a flatbread with toppings, and while modern traditional pizza traces its roots back to eighteenth-century Naples, within Italy itself—in Sicily, for example, where pizza is thick and rectangular—different kinds of pizzas have evolved in different places. (As of 2009, Naples pizza received the EU's Traditional Specialty Guarantee protection status.) The tomato,, a New World food that today seems inseparable from Italian cuisine, didn't arrive in Italy until the mid-sixteenth century. Pizza gained massively in popularity after World War II, when G.I.s who had been stationed in Italy returned to the U.S. with a taste for pizza. Thus, the modern pizza was born and continued to change over the twentieth century into the vibrant and diverse pizza culture we have today.

And without a doubt, today pizza is among America's favorite foods. It's certainly one of the most ubiquitous. It's part of my own roots as an Italian-American as well. Although this important food from Italy continues to evolve, even just within the American context, pizza can be a surprisingly hot-button topic, with arguments over authenticity and whether or not a topping even belongs on a pizza. Don't believe me? Try getting a New Yorker and a Chicagoan in the same room to duke it out over which is better, thin-crust or deep-dish pizza (or, for that matter, whether deep-dish pizza really *is* pizza). Or bring up the words "anchovy," "pineapple," "barbecued chicken," and "pizza" at your next dinner party and see where the conversation goes. The point is that we all have an opinion about an ingredient or style that we believe disqualifies a pizza from being a pizza. Fortunately, we don't need to settle these controversies, or have a universally accepted definition of pizza, in order to enjoy everything this wonderfully versatile food has to offer.

My goal has always been to create different, inspired pizzas, always pushing the envelope. As a professional chef, I know what satisfies my customers, and as a father, I know what's a crowd pleaser among the junior set. And so, with *Rustic Pizza*, I want to offer you my latest insights: new takes on old favorites as well as creative combinations. While there are many traditional red-sauce pizzas in this book, you'll find many other—and perhaps surprising—recipes that will have you thinking outside the (pizza delivery) box. Maybe it's the Roasted Pear, Camembert, and Watercress Pizza (see page 100) or the Kale and Chorizo Pizza (see page 155) or the Roasted Cauliflower and Bacon Pizza (see page 134). It's my hope that this book will help you push the boundaries of what pizza can be, and that soon, with a bit of practice, you'll start to combine flavors, textures, and toppings in your own way. If you've got kids, involve them in the process of measuring, mixing, watching the dough rise, and then decorating their own pizzas. It's a way of making cooking a family event and an opportunity to share and celebrate together in the best way possible—with great food.

When choosing toppings for your pizza, try to go for simple, seasonal, fresh ingredients that are local to your part of the world. Choose organic whenever you can, and get to know your local farmers market. It will fill you with ideas.

Another tip: Don't overload your pizza with sauce or toppings. Too much sauce in particular will make it soggy, and you won't get the crisp crust you're looking for. As I always say, when it comes to pizza, less is more!

With more than 100 individual pizza recipes, plus dozens of toppings and sauces that you can mix and match, *Rustic Pizza* offers virtually unlimited combinations. You can have a different pizza every night! While rustic pizzas are quick to assemble, they sometimes require a bit of prep to get all of those fabulous layers of flavor. Fear not—most of the topping prep is simple. Do that first, and once you finish, come back to your pizza recipe and you'll see that everything is simple and laid out on one page. Also, make use of your freezer: if you've got tomato sauce or pesto and a few prepped toppings in the freezer, and you pick up some prosciutto or roast chicken on the way home, a rustic pizza dinner could be just minutes away!

With the exception of the Sicilian-style pizzas in chapter 7, the recipes in this book make two pizzas, each serving one to two people. They only take a few minutes to cook, so have a glass of wine or a cold beer while you wait, and hang out in the kitchen chatting with your guests—make it a pizza party!

EQUIPMENT, TIPS, AND TRICKS

I don't want to place the bar for making good pizza too high, so I'm not going to suggest that you load up your kitchen with a lot of needless gadgets. However, there are a few key items that are good to have on hand. You might already own many of them.

BAKING STONE OR STEEL Almost every recipe in this book starts with preheating the oven with a baking stone in place.

A baking stone, also known as a pizza stone, is a large porous stone slab that helps mimic the conditions of a commercial pizza oven, though your home oven will never get as hot as a pizza oven—which can reach 800°F or more! Place the stone on the oven's bottom rack and bake the pizza directly on the stone. This will help maintain a steady oven temperature and produce a more pizzeria-like crust. Note that baking stones are fragile and prone to cracking due to sudden temperature changes, so you can't just stick one in a hot oven—the key is to start with a cold oven and give the stone a chance to heat gently all the way through.

To help avoid getting liquids or melted cheese on your baking stone (a nightmare to remove!) make sure you leave a wide enough raised lip (edge) on your pizzas, about 1 inch. (For special tips and techniques for baking gluten-free pizzas, see the notes on page 12.)

Instead of a dedicated baking stone, some people use unglazed terra-cotta or quarry tiles, which are available at hardware stores for a few bucks. But most traditional baking stones are quite affordable, in the $20 to $40 range. The downside is they break easily.

In response to some of the negatives of baking stones, in the last few years, baking steels have started appearing. These slabs of steel are meant to offer better heat conduction, more closely mimicking the conditions in commercial ovens, and, in turn, making better pizza. A baking steel obviously doesn't have the same breakage issues as a ceramic baking stone, but it does come with a higher price tag and is much heavier.

Here's another tip: If you're really nervous about placing the pizza directly on the stone and want a bit of practice before you take the plunge, I suggest you pick up an inexpensive 12-inch-round, metal (not cast iron) pizza pan that you can build the pizza on and just slide it on top of the stone. You won't get exactly the same texture for the crust, but you'll get close. The pizza pan is also quite useful for catching spills or wayward toppings.

PIZZA PEEL The pizza peel scares some people, even those with a great deal of cooking experience. If you're one of those people, try my earlier tip and bake the pizza on a thin pizza pan on top of a baking stone. But with a bit of practice, you, too, can master the pizza peel! Essentially, you're going to build each pizza right on top of it, and that means the peel somehow, *somehow* has to slide easily off the peel and onto the baking stone. The secret is to sprinkle the peel generously with flour, then transfer the rolled-out dough on top. Assemble the pizza according to the recipe instructions, then shake the peel lightly to ensure the pizza is moving freely *before* you try to slide it on top of the stone. The last thing you want is your toppings tumbling off on top of the hot stone!

8- TO 10-INCH CHEF'S KNIFE Classify rotary pizza cutters under "nice to have but not necessary." To cut a pizza, all you really need is a good chef's knife. It will last you a lifetime.

SHEET PAN If you're going to be making thick-crust, or Sicilian-style, pizzas, you'll want a good-quality half sheet pan (18 x 13 x 1 inch). Make sure that it is at least 1 inch deep to accommodate the olive oil needed for the Sicilian-style pizza dough.

STAND MIXER With a stand mixer and a hook attachment, you can make pizza dough in about 10 minutes, minus the rising time, of course.

CHEESE GRATERS A box grater is perfect for grating most of the cheeses used in this book, including mozzarella, Fontina, Gouda, Cheddar, and others. A microplane is a very handy rasp-style grater that quickly and easily grates small quantities of hard cheeses like Parmesan and Romano. You can also use it for grating zest, ginger, garlic, nutmeg, and more.

CUTTING BOARD When you take your pizza out of the oven, you'll want to transfer it to a stable, flat, and heat-resistant surface. A big wooden cutting board is ideal.

FOOD PROCESSOR A food processor makes quick work out of sauces like pesto and chimichurri, purées like my White Bean Hummus (see page 59) or Portobello Mushroom Purée (see page 56), and can even be used for grating larger amounts of Parmesan or Romano cheeses.

ROLLING PIN A rolling pin will help you get the pizza dough as thin as possible for that crispy crust. Be sure to flour it so it doesn't stick to the dough.

DOUGH CUTTER/SCRAPER A stainless-steel dough cutter is ideal for cutting the pizza dough into four even pieces. It can also be used to scrape up ingredients from a cutting board.

TONGS Long-handled tongs have innumerable uses in the kitchen. For making rustic pizza, they're great for grabbing a finished pizza to help slide it back on the peel and out of the oven.

OVEN Get to know your oven. When you set your oven to a certain temperature, that's the temperature the oven heats to, right? Not necessarily. Oven temperatures can vary widely. To make sure your oven reaches the correct temperature needed for the pizza recipes (usually around 500°F), check it with an oven thermometer.

The pizzas in this book are baked quickly at a relatively high heat—though not as quickly or as hot as in a pizza oven—so don't stray too far from the kitchen. You'll want to keep an eye on them as they cook. Your ideal pizza should be beautifully browned on the top and around the edge, not blackened.

When you first start out, try a few of the simpler recipes, like Oliver Pizza (see page 66), Margherita (see page 81), Bronx Bomber (see page 126), and Two-Sauce Pizza (see page 121), so that you can get comfortable with the pizza-making process in your own oven.

FREEZER Your freezer is your secret weapon for simplified pizza making. Freeze extra sauce in pizza-sized amounts that you can thaw quickly when the craving strikes. Make extra pizza dough to thaw in the fridge overnight for weeknight pizza. You can even freeze hard cheeses like Parmesan and Romano.

1
THE
DOUGH

The heart and soul of a good pizza is the crust, so I want you to start your rustic pizza journey here, with the dough, because it's so elemental. This chapter offers five pizza doughs: my time-tested and easy-to-make basic pizza dough and a healthy whole wheat version of it, a traditional Italian-style dough, a richer thick-crust (Sicilian-style) dough, and because I'm aware that many people who can't consume gluten still love pizza, a gluten-free dough. I want you to be able to get it right, so don't rush—take the time to get to know your dough.

BASIC PIZZA DOUGH

Many people are scared of yeast, but they shouldn't be. True, working with a yeast dough takes a bit of practice, but what good thing in life doesn't? If you're already comfortable working with bread doughs, you may notice that this dough is on the wet side, and that's exactly what you want for a thin-crust pizza that is both crispy and chewy. Once the dough hits the baking stone it will puff up. If you really don't want to make your own dough, go to your favorite local pizza shop and buy a piece of dough or look for premade dough at better supermarkets, and follow the steps below for rolling it out. But if you have the time, it's worth trying it from scratch. When measuring flour, make sure to lightly spoon it into the measuring cup and level it off. Don't stick the whole measuring cup into the bag of flour to scoop it or you could get a different measurement.

What's important to know about working with a yeast dough is that it's always different because yeast is alive—and that's kind of the magic of it. It can be affected by temperature and humidity. If you use the exact same quantities of ingredients on a warm, humid day then again on a cold, dry day, you could get different results, which is why making pizza dough takes practice. You'll learn to respond to what it needs—more flour, more water, another minute of kneading. That said, my dough is pretty forgiving. And while my basic pizza dough does call for using a stand mixer, you can absolutely make this the old-fashioned way and knead the dough by hand until it's smooth and elastic.

Most of the pizza recipes in this book make two 8- to 10-inch pizzas. If you're not using all four dough rounds at once, you can wrap them up and freeze them until the next time you make pizza. Thaw the dough in the refrigerator, but bring it to room temperature before using it.

MAKES ENOUGH DOUGH FOR 4 (8- TO 10-INCH) PIZZAS

¼ cup whole wheat flour

3½ cups all-purpose flour, plus additional for rolling

2 teaspoons (¼ ounce) instant yeast

2 teaspoons kosher salt

2 teaspoons sugar

2 teaspoons extra-virgin olive oil

1⅔ cups lukewarm water (105°F–110°F)

1 Line two sheet pans with parchment paper and set aside.

2 In the bowl of a stand mixer fitted with a dough hook, place the whole wheat and all-purpose flours, yeast, salt, and sugar.

3 With the mixer on low speed, slowly add the oil and then the water. Continue mixing on low until the dough is firm and smooth, about 10 minutes.

4 Divide the dough equally into four rounds. Place the dough rounds on the prepared sheet pans and cover them with a damp towel; let rise until doubled in size, about 2 hours.

5 To roll out the dough, generously flour your work surface and place one dough round on it. With floured fingers, press down in the center of the dough with the tips of your fingers, spreading the dough with your hands. When the dough has doubled in width, use a floured rolling pin to roll it out until it is very thin, like flatbread. The outer border should be a little thicker than the inner circle to make a sort of lip to hold in the sauce and toppings. Pick the dough up with a spatula or with the back of a knife, allowing it to fold up almost like an umbrella, and transfer it to a peel. Do not worry that the pizza is not round; you are looking for an 8- to 10-inch shape, a cross between an oval and a rectangle. If you get a hole, simply pinch it back together. Repeat with the remaining dough rounds and proceed with any of the pizza recipes.

ITALIAN-STYLE PIZZA DOUGH

Italian 00 (*doppio zero*, or "double zero") flour is a higher-protein, very finely ground, powdery soft flour. It is *the* traditional pizza flour. Dough made from 00 flour is a little stickier than dough made from all-purpose or bread flour. It requires less water, and if you find that the dough is not really coming together into a ball, you can add additional flour, 1 tablespoon at a time, but don't overdo it because you still want a relatively wet dough.

MAKES ENOUGH DOUGH FOR 4 (8- TO 10-INCH) PIZZAS

3¾ cups Italian "00" flour, plus additional for rolling

2 teaspoons (¼ ounce) instant yeast

2 teaspoons kosher salt

2 teaspoons sugar

2 teaspoons extra-virgin olive oil

1⅓ cups lukewarm water (105°F–110°F)

1 Line two sheet pans with parchment paper and set aside.

2 In the bowl of a stand mixer fitted with a dough hook, place the flour, yeast, salt, and sugar.

3 With the mixer on low speed, slowly add the oil and then the water. Continue mixing on low until the dough is firm and smooth, about 10 minutes.

4 Divide the dough equally into four rounds. Place the dough rounds on the prepared sheet pans and cover them with a damp towel; let rise until doubled in size, about 2 hours.

5 To roll out the dough, generously flour your work surface and place one dough round on it. With floured fingers, press down in the center of the dough with the tips of your fingers, spreading the dough with your hands. When the dough has doubled in width, use a floured rolling pin to roll it out until it is very thin, like flatbread. The outer border should be a little thicker than the inner circle to make a sort of lip to hold in the sauce and toppings. Pick the dough up with a spatula or with the back of a knife, allowing it to fold up almost like an umbrella, and transfer it to a peel. Do not worry that the pizza is not round; you are looking for an 8- to 10-inch shape, a cross between an oval and a rectangle. If you get a hole, simply pinch it back together. Repeat with the remaining dough rounds and proceed with any of the pizza recipes.

WHOLE WHEAT PIZZA DOUGH

For a whole wheat alternative to Basic Pizza Dough (see page 8), increase the amount of whole wheat flour to just under 50 percent. Whole wheat flour doughs absorb more water than regular wheat flour doughs. It can also take a little longer to rise, so be patient!

MAKES ENOUGH DOUGH FOR 4 (8- TO 10-INCH) PIZZAS

1¾ cups whole wheat flour

2 cups all-purpose flour, plus additional for rolling

2 teaspoons (¼ ounce) instant yeast

2 teaspoons kosher salt

2 teaspoons sugar

2 teaspoons extra-virgin olive oil

1⅔ cups lukewarm water (105°F–110°F), plus additional as needed

1 Line two sheet pans with parchment paper and set aside.

2 In the bowl of a stand mixer fitted with a dough hook, place the whole wheat and all-purpose flours, yeast, salt, and sugar.

3 With the mixer on low speed, slowly add the oil, then the water. Continue mixing on low until the dough is firm and smooth, about 10 minutes. If the dough seems dry, add more lukewarm water, 1 tablespoon at a time. If it seems wet, add more flour, 1 tablespoon at a time, until fully incorporated. The dough will be wet, but it will form into a ball.

4 Divide the dough equally into four rounds. Place the dough rounds on the prepared sheet pans and cover them with a damp towel; let rise until doubled in size, about 2 hours.

5 To roll out the dough, generously flour your work surface and place one dough round on it. With floured fingers, press down in the center of the dough with the tips of your fingers, spreading the dough with your hands. When the dough has doubled in width, use a floured rolling pin to roll it out until it is very thin, like flatbread. The outer border should be a little thicker than the inner circle to make a sort of lip to hold in the sauce and toppings. Pick the dough up with a spatula or with the back of a knife, allowing it to fold up almost like an umbrella, and transfer it to a peel. Do not worry that the pizza is not round; you are looking for an 8- to 10-inch shape, a cross between an oval and a rectangle. If you get a hole, simply pinch it back together. Repeat with the remaining dough rounds and proceed with any of the rustic pizza recipes.

GLUTEN-FREE PIZZA DOUGH

Many people with celiac disease or gluten intolerance tell me that pizza is by far the hardest food to give up. They miss and crave a good pizza, and while the commercially produced alternatives are improving every year, they still leave much to be desired. Why settle for less when you can make your own great gluten-free pizza dough? Now, you should know that working with gluten-free pizza dough is nothing like working with its "gluten-full" counterpart. You'll know you have the right consistency when it's like a thick pancake batter. Instead of rolling it out, use a spatula or wet fingertips to spread it out to your desired thickness. For best results, try to find a "one-to-one" gluten-free flour mix (my gluten-free pizza dough has been tested with King Arthur's Gluten Free Measure for Measure and Bob's Red Mill Gluten Free 1-to-1 Baking Flour). Such mixes have been specifically developed to substitute in recipes that usually contain gluten.

Just as with any yeast dough, gluten-free dough takes practice. If time is short, you can always substitute a commercially produced gluten-free crust to use with your favorite toppings, but this one is worth the effort to master. (The good news is it doesn't even require kneading.) Unlike regular pizza dough, gluten-free dough should be partially baked ("parbaked") before using. Leftover parbaked crusts can be frozen for up to two weeks.

Because it's a little trickier to form a lip on a gluten-free dough, I suggest you bake the pizzas at 450°F on parchment paper (one designed for high temperatures) on top of the baking stone or on a parchment paper-lined sheet pan. This will help to catch any escaped cheese, sauce, or toppings. This crust takes a bit longer to bake than a regular thin-crust pizza, anywhere from 10 to 14 minutes. Pull the pizza out of the oven as soon as it turns a nice golden brown.

MAKES ENOUGH DOUGH FOR 4 (8- TO 10-INCH) PIZZAS

2½ cups lukewarm water (105°F-110°F), more or less may be needed

1 tablespoon instant yeast

2 teaspoons honey or sugar

3½ cups gluten-free flour mix (see note above)

1 tablespoon cornmeal

2 teaspoons kosher salt

1 tablespoon extra-virgin olive oil

1 One hour before baking, place a baking stone in the oven and preheat it to 450°F.

2 Cut 4 sheets of parchment paper to fit the size of the baking stone and grease lightly.

3 In a Pyrex measuring cup, stir together 2 cups of the water with the yeast and honey. Set aside for 10 minutes, or until puffy and bubbling.

4 Meanwhile, in a large bowl, whisk together the flour, cornmeal, and salt. Pour in the yeast mixture and stir to combine. Add more lukewarm water, up to the remaining ½ cup, until the consistency is somewhere between a thick pancake batter and a cookie dough. Stir in the oil. Cover the dough tightly with plastic wrap and let it rest 30 to 60 minutes.

5 After the dough has rested, take a knife and draw an X shape in the dough to divide it into 4 pieces. Using a greased spatula or wet fingertips, spread one-fourth of the dough onto the parchment paper in a circular shape as thinly and evenly as possible.

6 Using a pizza peel, slide the dough onto the pizza stone. Parbake the dough for 10 to 12 minutes, or until it is just beginning to turn very light golden brown.

7 Repeat steps 5 and 6 using fresh parchment paper. Use the crust immediately, or cool it completely and then freeze it between sheets of wax paper for longer storage.

SICILIAN-STYLE PIZZA DOUGH

Sicilian style. Grandma pizza. Focaccia style. Whatever you call it, thick-crust pizza is comforting and delicious. You don't even need a baking stone; just use a basic sheet pan and you're set.

MAKES ENOUGH DOUGH FOR 1 (18 X 13-INCH) PIZZA

¼ cup whole wheat flour

3½ cups all-purpose flour

2 teaspoons (¼ ounce) instant yeast

2 teaspoons kosher salt

2 teaspoons sugar

2 teaspoons extra-virgin olive oil, plus
    ¼ cup olive oil for the pan

1⅔ cups lukewarm water (105°F–110°F)

1 In the bowl of a stand mixer fitted with a dough hook, place the whole wheat and all-purpose flours, yeast, salt, and sugar.

2 With the mixer on low speed, slowly add 2 teaspoons of the oil and then the water. Continue mixing on low until the dough is firm and smooth, about 10 minutes.

3 Transfer the dough to a lightly oiled bowl and cover it with a damp towel; let rise until doubled in size, about 2 hours.

4 Meanwhile, coat a half sheet pan with the remaining oil. Transfer the dough to the pan and gently stretch it to fit the pan. If the dough springs back, let it rest a few minutes before continuing. Dimple the surface gently with your fingertips.

5 Cover the pan with plastic wrap and let the dough rise, 30 to 40 minutes, before proceeding with one of the pizza recipes.

Note: You need to use a rimmed half sheet pan (at least 1 inch deep) to hold the olive oil used in step 4; a cookie sheet will not work for this purpose.

2
SAUCES AND FLAVORED OILS

When you think about some of the most memorable pizzas you've tasted, chances are the sauce was a big part of the flavor. Maybe it was a little spicy or had a hint of sweetness or tasted just of fresh tomatoes. In this chapter I offer a range of classic sauces and flavored oils (which is not to say that every pizza needs a sauce, as you'll soon see!), some to top the crust, others to drizzle on the finished pizza to pull all of the flavors together.

MARINARA SAUCE

Most pizzas use some version of marinara sauce. Mine is simpler than you might think—the only seasonings are a little onion, garlic, and basil. You really don't need anything else. On a pizza, you're working with multiple layers of flavor, so you want the sauce to play along like an instrument in an orchestra, not be a soloist. Always buy the best-quality canned tomatoes you can find. Use leftover sauce for pasta night or freeze it in small portions for your next pizzas.

MAKES ABOUT 4 CUPS

3 tablespoons extra-virgin olive oil

1 tablespoon minced white onion

1 clove garlic, minced

1 (28-ounce) can whole tomatoes in juice

1¼ teaspoons kosher salt

½ teaspoon freshly ground black pepper

1½ tablespoons chopped fresh basil leaves

1 In a large pot over medium heat, heat the oil until hot. Add the onion and cook until it is translucent, 2 to 3 minutes. Stir in the garlic and cook until fragrant, about 30 seconds. Crush the tomatoes with your hands, discarding any tough pieces, and add them to the pot, along with their juice. Stir in the salt, pepper, and basil.

2 Increase the heat to high and bring the mixture to a boil. Lower the heat to a simmer, cover, and cook for about 1 hour, stirring occasionally. Taste and adjust the seasoning, if needed. For a smoother texture, pulse the sauce briefly in a food processor.

ROASTED TOMATO SAUCE

Dinners made in sheet pans are all the rage, and this is like sheet pan sauce! It's even easier than a regular tomato sauce because you just throw all the ingredients together in a roasting pan, stick it in the oven, and about 1 hour later you have a sauce. For a smoother texture, pulse the sauce in the food processor. As with the Marinara Sauce (see page 16), you can freeze this in smaller portions that are the perfect quantity for one or two pizzas.

MAKES ABOUT 7 CUPS

3 pounds fresh plum tomatoes, or
    2 (28-ounce) cans whole tomatoes in
    juice, well drained

½ cup chicken broth or water

1 large Spanish onion, peeled and sliced

½ cup fresh basil leaves

⅓ cup extra-virgin olive oil

2 teaspoons kosher salt

½ to 1 teaspoon freshly ground
    black pepper

1 Preheat the oven to 375°F.

2 In a roasting pan, toss all the ingredients together to combine. Bake until the tomato skins are charred and the sauce has just begun to come together, 45 to 60 minutes.

3 When the mixture is cool enough to handle, coarsely chop the tomatoes. Be sure to scrape up the pan juices.

BOLOGNESE SAUCE

A decadent choice atop a meat lover's pizza, classic Bolognese is a delicious, slow-cooked meat sauce, sometimes known as ragù. It's comfort cooking at its finest, perfect for a lazy Sunday afternoon when you have the time to stir occasionally as the sauce bubbles away, making your home smell wonderful. You can add a little additional liquid, such as stock or water, if the sauce gets too dry, but it should be thick and meaty.

MAKES ABOUT 3 CUPS

1 tablespoon extra-virgin olive oil

1 pound meatloaf mix (equal parts beef, pork, and veal)

¼ cup diced carrot

¼ cup diced celery

¼ cup diced onion

2 cloves garlic, thinly sliced

1 small pinch cinnamon

1 bay leaf

½ cup whole milk

1 (14.5-ounce) can diced tomatoes

Kosher salt

1 In a large pot over medium heat, heat the oil until hot. Add the meatloaf mix and cook until browned, about 5 minutes. Drain well and set the meat aside in a bowl.

2 To the same pot, add the carrot, celery, onion, garlic, cinnamon, and bay leaf and sauté on medium heat, stirring occasionally, until the vegetables are softened, 8 to 10 minutes.

3 Stir in the milk, and cook for 1 to 2 minutes more. Add the reserved meatloaf mix and the tomatoes. Season with salt and bring the mixture to a boil. Cover, reduce the heat to low, and cook, stirring occasionally, 3 to 4 hours.

FRESH TOMATO SAUCE

This is the easiest tomato sauce ever! You don't even have to cook it. Just toss the ingredients into a food processor and press pulse. Fresh tomato sauce is ideal for any pizza where you really want the taste of the tomato and toppings to come through, such as pizzas with fresh mozzarella and fresh vegetables. The key here is to leave the sauce with a little bit of texture—don't go for an entirely smooth purée.

MAKES ABOUT 3 CUPS

1 (28-ounce) can whole tomatoes in juice, well drained

1 clove garlic, chopped

¼ cup extra-virgin olive oil

1 teaspoon kosher salt

Freshly ground black pepper

In a food processor, pulse together the tomatoes, garlic, oil, salt, and pepper to taste until the ingredients are combined. Taste and adjust the seasoning, if needed.

ALMOND PESTO

Almond Pesto replaces the traditional pine nuts with toasted almonds and uses just a touch of Parmesan, making the basil the real star.

MAKES ½ CUP TO ¾ CUP

¼ cup almonds, toasted

2 cloves garlic, roughly chopped

2 cups tightly packed fresh basil leaves

¼ cup plus 2 tablespoons extra-virgin olive oil

1 teaspoon freshly grated Parmesan cheese

½ teaspoon kosher salt

1 In a food processor, pulse together the almonds and garlic until the ingredients are well chopped. Add the basil and pulse until it is chopped. While the machine is running, gradually add the oil and process until the mixture is smooth.

2 Transfer the mixture to a small bowl and stir in the Parmesan and salt. Use immediately, or freeze.

TRADITIONAL BASIL PESTO

A basic pesto recipe is a must for every cook. It's delicious, simple to make, and superior to any store-bought version. If you've only ever had tomato sauce on pizza, using pesto should be your next step; it will open up a whole world of options for creating delicious varieties of pizzas. Leftover pesto can be tossed with pasta, used as a sandwich spread, or simply frozen in small portions until the next time you make pizza.

MAKES ABOUT 1 CUP

¼ cup pine nuts

2 cloves garlic, roughly chopped

2 cups tightly packed fresh basil leaves

¼ cup plus 2 tablespoons extra-virgin olive oil

½ cup freshly grated Parmesan cheese (or a combination of Parmesan and Pecorino Romano cheeses)

Kosher salt

1 In a food processor, pulse together the pine nuts and garlic until they are well chopped. Add the basil and pulse until it is chopped. While the machine is running, gradually add the oil and process until the mixture is smooth.

2 Transfer the mixture to a small bowl and stir in the Parmesan. Season with salt. Use immediately, or freeze.

ROMESCO SAUCE

Romesco sauce is a very special and delicious Spanish sauce that uses almonds and red pepper as a flavor base. It is traditionally served with fish. In Spain, it can be found in many variations. This simple, smoky version can be whipped up in a few minutes in the blender or food processor and doesn't require roasting tomatoes or peppers. Use on vegetable- or seafood-based pizzas.

MAKES ABOUT 1¼ CUPS

½ cup slivered almonds, toasted

1 (6.7-ounce) jar piquillo peppers, or 1 large roasted red pepper

2 medium tomatoes, seeded, cored, and roughly chopped

¼ cup extra-virgin olive oil

2 cloves garlic, roughly chopped

¼ teaspoon pimentón (smoked Spanish paprika)

¼ teaspoon red pepper flakes

1 to 2 teaspoons sherry vinegar

Kosher salt and freshly ground black pepper

1 In a food processor, process together the almonds, peppers, tomatoes, oil, garlic, pimentón, and red pepper flakes until the mixture is smooth.

2 Transfer the mixture to a bowl and stir in the vinegar. Season with salt and pepper.

ROASTED GARLIC BÉCHAMEL

Béchamel is a classic white sauce. It is a wonderful base for other flavors—in this case, roasted garlic—but you can also add cheese to make a cheese sauce. If you don't have the roasted garlic on hand, don't let that stop you from making the sauce: either leave the garlic out to make a basic béchamel or throw in 1 minced clove in step 2. If the sauce seems too thick after storing and reheating, add a little milk to thin it to the desired consistency. The secret is to whisk continuously.

MAKES 1 CUP

1 cup whole milk

4 teaspoons unsalted butter

1 tablespoon (3 to 4 cloves) chopped or mashed Roasted Garlic (see page 36)

1 tablespoon all-purpose flour

½ teaspoon kosher salt

⅛ teaspoon ground nutmeg

Freshly ground black pepper

1 In a small saucepan on low heat, heat the milk until warm. Alternatively, you can microwave the milk for 1 minute. Keep it warm while you make the roux (the flour and butter mixture).

2 In a medium saucepan over medium heat, melt the butter. Add the flour and whisk until the roux turns golden brown, 3 to 4 minutes. Slowly stir in the hot milk and garlic, whisking continuously until smooth. Bring the mixture to a boil, reduce the heat to low, and cook until thickened, 2 to 3 minutes, whisking constantly. Remove from the heat and stir in the salt and nutmeg. Season with pepper.

3 Use the sauce immediately, or cover it by lightly pressing plastic wrap against its surface to avoid a skin forming, and refrigerate.

CHIMICHURRI SAUCE

Chimichurri is an extremely versatile, easy, and tasty sauce that is sure to become one of your go-to favorites for all kinds of dishes. This herby, garlicky Argentinian sauce is often used to dress or marinate meat, particularly flank and skirt steaks. Some versions are made with just parsley, but this one combines cilantro and parsley for a well-rounded flavor. If you're cilantro-averse, use all parsley. Drizzle chimichurri on finished meat-based pizzas for a bright, slightly acidic and herbal contrast. Leftovers can be spooned over beef, chicken, or fish, used as a marinade, or even served over potatoes or other vegetables.

MAKES ABOUT ½ CUP

½ cup packed cilantro leaves and stems

½ cup packed parsley leaves and stems

2 cloves garlic, roughly chopped

¼ teaspoon red pepper flakes

⅓ cup extra-virgin olive oil, plus more as needed

1½ teaspoons freshly squeezed lime juice

1½ teaspoons red or white wine vinegar

Kosher salt

---

1 In a food processor, pulse together the cilantro, parsley, garlic, and red pepper flakes until the ingredients are chopped. While the machine is running, gradually add the oil and process until the mixture is smooth.

2 Transfer the mixture to a small bowl and stir in the lime juice and vinegar. Season with salt.

TOMATO OIL

Drizzle this flavorful oil on finished pizzas for the essence of roasted tomato and garlic.

MAKES ABOUT 1 CUP

¼ cup cherry tomatoes

5 cloves garlic, unpeeled

2 tablespoons chopped roasted red pepper from a jar

1 teaspoon chopped fresh oregano

1 anchovy fillet, rinsed if salt packed

½ bay leaf

¼ teaspoon red pepper flakes

1 cup olive oil

Kosher salt

1 Heat the broiler with the oven rack 6 inches from the heating element. Place the tomatoes and garlic on a sheet pan and broil, turning occasionally, until blistered and brown, 5 to 8 minutes. Let sit until cool enough to handle. Peel the garlic cloves.

2 In a small bowl, mix together all of the ingredients except the salt. Let sit for 1 hour to allow the flavors to infuse.

3 Remove the bay leaf and transfer the mixture to a food processor. Pulse until a chunky purée forms. Season with salt. Strain the purée through a fine-mesh strainer. The oil is ready to use.

BASIL OIL

This basil-infused oil comes together in just a few minutes. Use it as a finishing oil, or add a tablespoon or two to one of the tomato sauces for instant fresh basil flavor.

MAKES ABOUT 1½ CUPS

1 small clove garlic, minced

1 cup fresh basil leaves

1 cup extra-virgin olive oil

½ teaspoon kosher salt

¼ teaspoon freshly ground black pepper

In a food processor, pulse together the garlic and basil until the ingredients are chopped. Add the oil, salt, and pepper and process until the mixture is smooth.

MINT OIL

Drizzle mint oil on finished pizzas and flatbreads with Mediterranean and Middle Eastern flavors. Try it with Tahini Sauce (see page 29) and Baba Ghanoush (see page 53). Stir a little into Herbed Yogurt Sauce (see page 32) or Tzatziki Sauce (see page 30).

MAKES ⅔ TO ¾ CUP

3 to 4 tablespoons fresh Italian flat-leaf parsley

Generous ½ cup fresh mint leaves

⅓ cup vegetable oil

2 tablespoons olive oil

¼ teaspoon kosher salt

Freshly ground black pepper

In a food processor, pulse together the parsley and mint until the ingredients are chopped. Add the vegetable and olive oils, salt, and a pinch of pepper and process until the mixture is smooth.

TAHINI SAUCE

Tahini is a thick paste made from ground sesame seeds. It's one of the main ingredients in hummus, but it can also be made into a simple sauce when thinned with water and flavored with lemon and garlic. Before you measure the tahini, make sure that you stir it well, because it separates. Drizzle tahini sauce on finished vegetable pizzas. Leftovers are great on roasted vegetables.

MAKES ABOUT 1 CUP

1 clove garlic, minced

2 to 3 tablespoons freshly squeezed lemon juice, or to taste

½ cup tahini (sesame seed paste), well stirred

Kosher salt

1 Whisk together the garlic and lemon juice. Stir in the tahini; the mixture will be thick.

2 Begin adding water, up to ½ cup, a little at a time, and continue whisking until the mixture is the consistency of a thin pancake batter. It should drizzle easily off the spoon. Season with salt.

TZATZIKI SAUCE

Similar to Herbed Yogurt Sauce (see page 32) but thicker, tzatziki is a classic sauce made with Greek yogurt and cucumber.

MAKES JUST OVER 1 CUP

1 cup Greek yogurt

1 teaspoon freshly squeezed lemon juice

1 clove garlic, minced

¼ cup peeled, seeded, and chopped English or regular cucumber

2 tablespoons minced fresh herbs (any combination of parsley, dill, or mint)

2 teaspoons extra-virgin olive oil

Whole milk, as needed

Kosher salt and freshly ground black pepper

In a small bowl, stir together the yogurt, lemon juice, garlic, cucumber, herbs, and oil until combined. If too thick, thin the mixture with milk. Season with salt and pepper.

HERBED YOGURT SAUCE

Herbed Yogurt Sauce will enhance any Middle Eastern-inspired pizza or flatbread, and it also has a nice cooling effect over spice-rich foods.

MAKES 1 CUP

1 cup whole-milk yogurt (not Greek yogurt)

Juice of ½ lemon or lime

1 clove garlic, minced

¼ cup minced fresh herbs (any combination of parsley, dill, or mint)

Kosher salt and freshly ground black pepper

In a small bowl, stir together the yogurt, lemon juice, garlic, and herbs until combined. Season with salt and pepper.

SALSA VERDE

Many different cultures have a "green sauce." Italian-style salsa verde uses anchovies and capers for bold flavor. Even if you don't like anchovies, give this a try because the anchovy flavor fades into the sauce. Drizzle salsa verde on seafood or vegetable pizzas just out of the oven.

MAKES ABOUT ½ CUP

1 cup roughly chopped parsley, or a combination of parsley, cilantro, and mint

1 large clove garlic, coarsely chopped

⅓ cup extra-virgin olive oil

4 anchovy fillets, rinsed if salt packed

1 tablespoon capers

1 teaspoon white vinegar

1 teaspoon freshly squeezed lemon juice

½ teaspoon Dijon mustard

In a food processor, process together all the ingredients until they are smooth. Taste and adjust the seasoning, if needed, but you will probably not need to add salt because of the saltiness of the capers and anchovies.

MUSTARD AIOLI

Even though some food enthusiasts believe aiolis to be complicated, this mustard aioli is actually very easy to make. It's delicious and tangy, and great when drizzled on pizzas just out of the oven.

MAKES ABOUT 1¼ CUPS

1 clove garlic

2 tablespoons freshly squeezed lemon juice

2 large egg yolks

1 cup olive oil

2 to 3 tablespoons Dijon mustard

½ teaspoon kosher salt

1 pinch freshly ground black pepper

1 In a food processor, pulse the garlic until chopped. Add the lemon juice and egg yolks and process until the ingredients are well incorporated.

2 While the machine is running, gradually add the oil in a thin, steady stream and process until smooth. Add the mustard, salt, pepper, and 1 teaspoon of water and process until the mixture is thickened.

3 Transfer the mixture to a jar. Cover and refrigerate for at least 1 hour or up to 1 day.

Note: Raw eggs always carry a risk of foodborne illness and should not be served to young children, pregnant women, the elderly, and anyone with a compromised immune system. If you're squeamish about using them, many supermarkets now fortunately carry pasteurized eggs.

3

TOPPINGS

Toppings are the fun part. They give you the opportunity to be creative and try different things, such as new flavor combinations, building on the traditional pizza styles we know and love. Nowadays we're very lucky to have access to so many great ingredients that would have been considered exotic or rare as recently as twenty years ago. Of course, there are plenty of toppings that don't need any preparation, like prosciutto, olives, or sliced onions, but this chapter helps you build layers of flavors (and often nutrition) with ingredients like roasted eggplant or butternut squash, caramelized onions, grilled zucchini, sautéed kale, and much, much more.

ROASTED GARLIC

Sweet and nutty, roasted garlic is a deliciously mellow alternative to fresh garlic, and it couldn't be simpler to make. To use, just squeeze the soft, roasted garlic out of its peel and add it to pizzas, pastas, and more.

MAKES 2 HEADS GARLIC

2 heads garlic, unpeeled, tops sliced off

2 tablespoons olive oil

½ teaspoon kosher salt

½ teaspoon freshly ground black pepper

1 Preheat the oven to 400°F.

2 Place the garlic in a small baking dish and toss it with the oil, salt, and pepper.

3 Roast, uncovered, until the garlic is lightly browned and soft, about 25 minutes.

BALSAMIC ONIONS

The sweet and sour notes of Balsamic Onions add a depth of flavor to pizza that you wouldn't get with either ingredient used alone.

MAKES 1½ TO 2 CUPS

3½ cups balsamic vinegar

½ cup sugar

3 pounds Roasted Red Onions
(see below)

1 In a medium saucepan, heat the vinegar and sugar over medium-high heat until the liquid is reduced by half, about 20 minutes. Add the onions and cook until the liquid is syrupy, about 10 minutes.

2 Use immediately, or cover and refrigerate for up to 1 week.

ROASTED RED ONIONS

Roasted Red Onions are sweet, savory, caramelized—and perfect for pizza. Leftovers can be tossed with pasta, stirred into soup, or even added to salads.

MAKES 1½ TO 2 CUPS

3 pounds red onions, peeled and diced

3 tablespoons vegetable or canola oil

1 tablespoon kosher salt

1 tablespoon plus ½ teaspoon freshly ground black pepper

1 Preheat the oven to 350°F.

2 Place all the ingredients on a sheet pan and toss to coat the onions.

3 Roast until the onions are translucent, about 40 minutes, stirring occasionally to prevent blackening.

CARAMELIZED ONIONS

Almost everyone loves caramelized onions, and making a big batch of them is a snap. You just need to stay near the stove to stir them to ensure even cooking. In addition to using them as a topping for pizza, try them on bruschetta and sandwiches, and in pasta dishes, dips, soups, and more. They're so good you might want to eat them straight up with a sprinkle of sea salt!

MAKES 1½ TO 2 CUPS

1½ tablespoons unsalted butter

¼ cup vegetable or canola oil

3 pounds Spanish onions, peeled and thinly sliced

1 Place the butter and oil in a large skillet over medium heat. When the butter has melted, add the onions and stir. It is important to let the onions sweat before they start to caramelize, so reduce the heat if they are browning too fast. Cook, stirring regularly, until they are perfectly browned (not light but not too dark), about 40 minutes.

2 Use immediately, or cover and refrigerate for up to 2 days.

ROASTED BUTTERNUT SQUASH

With its sweet taste and smooth texture, butternut squash is an American favorite. Roasting brings out its natural sugars, which caramelize into sticky goodness. I don't give exact measurements here because you can use whatever size squash you can find. You may find it surprising as a pizza topping, but it's delicious in combination with cheese, herbs (particularly sage and thyme), cured pork products like pancetta and bacon, and much more. Give it a try!

MAKES 1 SQUASH

1 butternut squash, peeled, seeds and fibers removed, and cut into ½-inch pieces

Olive or canola oil, for coating

Kosher salt and freshly ground pepper

1 Preheat the oven to 400°F.

2 In a large bowl, toss the butternut squash pieces with enough oil to coat them; season with salt and pepper.

3 Evenly spread the pieces out in a single layer on a sheet pan. Roast until they are tender and caramelized, 25 to 30 minutes, occasionally turning them with a spatula.

BRAISED FENNEL

For a sublime and elegant pizza, add braised fennel. Braising brings out fennel's natural sweetness and softens its already delicate licorice flavors. On pizza, braised fennel pairs extremely well with Italian sausage, which is also usually flavored with fennel seeds. Squeeze out the excess liquid from the cooked fennel before using it to keep your pizza crust crispy!

MAKES ABOUT 1½ CUPS

2 tablespoons olive oil

2 bulbs fennel, trimmed and sliced into ¼-inch-thick slices

¼ cup white wine

¼ cup chicken or vegetable stock

Kosher salt and freshly ground black pepper

1 In a large skillet, heat the oil over medium-high heat until hot. Add the fennel in a single layer and cook until it is lightly browned on both sides, 4 to 5 minutes, lowering the heat if it begins to brown too quickly.

2 Deglaze the pan with the white wine, using a wooden spoon to scrape up any brown bits. Add the stock and season with salt and pepper. Cover the pan and reduce the heat to low. Cook until the fennel is tender, 10 to 12 minutes.

3 Remove the lid, and if there's still a lot of liquid in the pan, raise the heat and cook until most of the excess liquid has evaporated.

HERBED GOAT OR RICOTTA CHEESE

It's amazing how just a few teaspoons of herbs will liven up goat or ricotta cheese—and any pizza you dollop this delicious cheese onto. You can vary the herbs, if you like; chives, tarragon, and parsley would also be delicious. Leftovers can be used on salads and even as a sandwich spread.

MAKES 1 CUP

1 cup goat or ricotta cheese, at room temperature

1 teaspoon chopped fresh rosemary leaves

1 teaspoon chopped fresh sage leaves

1 teaspoon chopped fresh oregano leaves

Kosher salt and freshly ground black pepper

In a small bowl, stir together all the ingredients until well combined. Season with salt, if needed, and pepper.

ROASTED CHERRY TOMATOES

Roasted tomatoes are a classic Italian favorite. To make roasted cherry tomatoes, substitute 1½ pounds of cherry tomatoes for the plum tomatoes and reduce the cooking time to around 2 hours. These tomatoes are so delicious you'll want to eat them like candy.

MAKES 12 TOMATOES

12 plum tomatoes

1 to 2 tablespoons olive oil

1 teaspoon kosher salt

½ teaspoon freshly ground black pepper

1 Preheat the oven to 250°F.

2 Place the tomatoes on a sheet pan and rub them with the oil. Sprinkle the salt and pepper over the top.

3 Roast until the tomatoes are shriveled and slightly darkened, about 3 hours.

ROASTED BEETS

Roasting does something magical to beets, and even beet haters can become converts. Be sure to scrub your beets well before wrapping them. Any extra beets you don't use on a pizza can be used in salads. The quantity of beets to roast is entirely up to you. You could roast a single beet if you wanted to, but you may discover that you can't get enough of them!

1 to 2 pounds red or golden beets,
 trimmed of their ends and scrubbed

1 Preheat the oven to 425°F.

2 Wrap the beets individually in foil and place them on a sheet pan.

3 Bake for 45 minutes, or until they are tender (a knife should easily pierce through to the center).

4 When the beets are cool enough to handle, slip off the skins and slice the beets according to the recipe instructions.

WALNUT GORGONZOLA

In addition to using Walnut Gorgonzola on pizzas, try spooning this flavor-packed topping on salads, burgers, and more.

MAKES ABOUT 1 CUP

2 tablespoons extra-virgin olive oil

½ cup chopped walnuts

½ red onion, peeled and thinly sliced

2 tablespoons chopped fresh basil leaves

1 tablespoon balsamic vinegar

½ teaspoon kosher salt

3 ounces Gorgonzola cheese

¼ cup light or heavy cream

1 In a large skillet over medium heat, heat the oil until hot. Add the walnuts and cook until they are browned, 2 to 3 minutes. Transfer the walnuts to a small bowl and allow them to cool to room temperature. When cool, stir in the onion, basil, vinegar, and salt.

2 In a food processor, process together the Gorgonzola and cream until the mixture is smooth. Stir this mixture into the walnut mixture.

ROASTED EGGPLANT

A staple of Italian cuisine, roasted eggplant is a nutritious and tasty pizza topping you may not have considered. While it's not strictly necessary to salt an eggplant to remove bitterness, it's often helpful to do so if your eggplant is particularly large. If you wish to salt it, toss the slices with some kosher salt, then let them sit in a colander over a glass bowl for 1 hour before using them. Firmly pat the slices dry with paper towels to remove excess salt and moisture before proceeding.

1 eggplant, sliced into ½-inch-thick slices

Extra-virgin olive oil, for coating

Kosher salt and freshly ground black pepper

1 Preheat the oven to 400°F.

2 In a large bowl, toss the eggplant slices with enough oil to coat them. Toss with salt (omit the salt if you previously salted the eggplant) and pepper.

3 Evenly spread them out in a single layer on a sheet pan and roast them until browned and tender, about 20 to 30 minutes, turning the slices over once during baking.

CRISPY EGGPLANT

If you like eggplant parmesan, you'll love putting Crispy Eggplant on pizza. The secret is to slice the eggplant very thinly so it browns up quickly. Use the slices soon after cooking so that they keep their crunch.

½ cup Italian-style bread crumbs

2 tablespoons finely chopped fresh basil

2 cloves garlic, minced

Vegetable oil, for deep frying

2 large eggs, beaten

¼ cup all-purpose flour

1 small eggplant (6 to 8 ounces), thinly sliced

Kosher salt and freshly ground black pepper

1 In a shallow bowl, stir together the bread crumbs, basil, and garlic. Place the eggs and the flour in two separate shallow bowls.

2 Heat about 1 inch of oil in a large heavy pan. Season the eggplant slices lightly with salt and pepper. Working in batches, dip the eggplant slices in the flour, then the egg, then the bread crumbs.

3 Transfer the slices to the pan, being careful not to crowd them. Fry until they are crispy and golden brown, then transfer them to a paper towel-lined plate to drain. Repeat with any remaining slices.

GRILLED ZUCCHINI

Zucchini is a wonderful, healthy, and easy-to-find ingredient that also works great as a pizza topping. Be sure to grill the zucchini slices right after you prepare them in step 1. Otherwise the salt will cause the zucchini to release water and you won't achieve a good sear. If you'd rather roast the zucchini slices, prepare them as in step 1 and bake in a 425°F oven for 20 to 25 minutes, or until golden brown.

MAKES ABOUT 1 CUP

1 medium zucchini, sliced into ¼-inch-thick slices

Olive oil, for coating

Kosher salt and freshly ground black pepper

1 In a medium bowl, toss together the zucchini slices with enough oil to coat them; season with salt and pepper.

2 Preheat a ridged grill pan over medium-high heat. Working in batches if necessary, add the zucchini slices in a single layer and cook for about 3 minutes, or until nice golden sear marks appear on the undersides. Flip and cook for another 2 minutes.

ROASTED PEARS

Pears on pizza? Why not? Pears are, in fact, amazing as a pizza topping—and they're way better than pineapple on pizza, if you ask me. Sometimes it pays to think outside the box. For centuries, Europeans have "paired" (pun intended) pears with many ingredients: cheeses, such as Gorgonzola and Camembert; cured meats, such as prosciutto and Jamón Serrano; a drizzle of balsamic vinegar; and many other delicious combinations. Pears just take your pizza to the next level!

MAKES 2 PEARS

2 Bosc or Bartlett pears, unpeeled and quartered

3 tablespoons olive oil

½ teaspoon kosher salt

¼ teaspoon freshly ground black pepper

1 Preheat the oven to 400°F.

2 In a large bowl, toss together all the ingredients until well combined. Evenly spread the pears out in a single layer on a sheet pan and roast them until they are tender but not limp, 15 to 20 minutes. Set aside to cool.

SAUTÉED MUSHROOMS

Sautéed mushrooms offer a whole different flavor profile on a pizza than raw mushrooms.

MAKES 1 TO 1¼ CUPS

1 tablespoon olive oil

1 clove garlic, minced

8 ounces cremini or white button mushrooms, sliced

Kosher salt and freshly ground pepper

1 In a large skillet over medium heat, heat the oil until hot. Add the garlic and sauté it until fragrant, about 30 seconds.

2 Add the mushrooms and cook, stirring occasionally, until they are browned, 6 to 8 minutes. It may look like they need more oil, but once the mushrooms start to release their liquid, you'll see that 1 tablespoon will be plenty.

3 Season lightly with salt and pepper.

SAUTÉED SPICY SPINACH

Tasty, healthy, and surprisingly elegant as a pizza topping, sautéed spinach is an easy ingredient that can be made spicy or not. To make regular sautéed spinach, just leave out the red pepper flakes.

MAKES ABOUT ½ CUP

1 tablespoon extra-virgin olive oil

4 garlic cloves, thinly sliced

¼ teaspoon red pepper flakes

8 ounces baby spinach leaves (about 6 cups)

⅛ teaspoon kosher salt

⅛ teaspoon freshly ground black pepper

In a large skillet over medium heat, heat the oil until hot. Add the garlic, red pepper flakes, and spinach and cook until the spinach is wilted, about 2 minutes. Sprinkle with the salt and black pepper. Set aside.

SAUTÉED KALE

A trendy and certainly nutritious ingredient, kale can be delicious on pizza when you treat it right. Sauté it in stock until it becomes tender, then reduce the liquid. Squeeze out any excess liquid to avoid a soggy crust.

MAKES ABOUT ½ CUP

1 tablespoon extra-virgin olive oil

4 garlic cloves, thinly sliced

8 ounces baby kale

½ cup chicken or vegetable stock

Kosher salt and freshly ground black pepper

1 In a large pan over medium heat, heat the oil until hot. Add the garlic and sauté it until it is lightly golden brown.

2 Add the kale and stock and cook until the kale is tender, 3 to 4 minutes. Turn up the heat to reduce the liquid. Season with salt and pepper.

SPICY AND GARLICKY BROCCOLINI

A cross between broccoli and Chinese kale, broccolini (aka baby broccoli) is a delicious, mild alternative to regular broccoli. It comes in individual long stems and will probably even make a convert of the broccoli haters in your life. Don't like spicy? Leave out the jalapeño.

MAKES ABOUT 2 CUPS

1 (8-ounce) package broccolini, trimmed

1 tablespoon olive oil

3 cloves garlic, thinly sliced

½ jalapeño pepper, seeded and thinly sliced (optional)

Kosher salt

1 Bring a large pot of water to a boil. Blanch the broccolini until tender, 2 to 3 minutes. Drain and rinse them under cold water to stop the cooking. Set aside.

2 In a medium skillet over medium heat, heat the oil until hot. Add the garlic and jalapeño, if using, and cook until the garlic is lightly golden, being careful not to burn it. Add the drained broccolini and toss until it is well coated and hot, about 2 minutes. Season with salt.

BABA GHANOUSH

Baba ghanoush is a delicious roasted eggplant dip. It's a bit unconventional as a pizza topping, but consider it a shortcut to major flavor. For even more flavor, finish a pizza made with baba ghanoush with Mint Oil (see page 28), Tahini Sauce (see page 29), or Herbed Yogurt Sauce (see page 32) as soon as it comes out of the oven.

MAKES ABOUT 1 CUP

1 tablespoon olive oil

1 large eggplant, pricked with a fork

1 clove garlic

2 tablespoons tahini (sesame seed paste)

2 tablespoons freshly squeezed lemon juice

1 tablespoon chopped fresh mint

½ teaspoon kosher salt

¼ teaspoon freshly ground black pepper

1 to 2 teaspoons lemon zest

¼ cup minced scallions

¼ cup chopped fresh cilantro leaves

1 Preheat the oven to 425°F.

2 Rub the oil on the eggplant, place it on a sheet pan, and roast, turning often, until it is very soft when pierced with a fork, about 45 minutes. For a smokier flavor, the eggplant can be grilled or cooked directly over a gas flame. (Always exercise care when cooking with fire!) Set aside to cool.

3 When the eggplant is cool enough to handle, scoop out its flesh and discard the skin. Place the garlic in a food processor and pulse until it is finely chopped. Add the eggplant and tahini and pulse to combine them.

4 Add the lemon juice, mint, salt, and pepper and pulse to combine them. Stir in the lemon zest, scallions, and cilantro. Cover the mixture and refrigerate it for at least 1 hour and up to overnight.

CAULIFLOWER PURÉE

Rich and delicious, this cauliflower purée is a surprisingly luxurious way to get your veggies. Use it as a base for cauliflower pizzas or other delicately flavored pies.

MAKES ABOUT 2 CUPS

½ head cauliflower, trimmed, cored, and cut into florets

2 cups heavy cream

1 to 2 cloves Roasted Garlic (see page 36) (optional)

Kosher salt and freshly ground black pepper

1 In a medium saucepan, add the florets, cream, and roasted garlic, if using; season with salt and pepper. Bring the mixture to a boil, then lower the heat to a simmer. Cook until the florets are tender, about 20 minutes.

2 Drain the florets, reserving the cooking liquid. Transfer the florets to a blender and add enough of the cooking liquid to emulsify them into a thick purée. Taste and adjust the seasoning, if needed.

ROASTED CAULIFLOWER

Roasting transforms cauliflower—admittedly a fairly bland vegetable when raw—into something sweet, crunchy, and delicious.

MAKES ABOUT 4 CUPS

1 (about 2-pound) head cauliflower, trimmed, cored, and cut into florets

2 tablespoons extra-virgin olive oil, plus more if needed

Kosher salt and freshly ground black pepper

1 Preheat the oven to 400°F.

2 In a 9 x 13-inch baking dish, toss the florets with the oil and season with salt and pepper.

3 Roast about 25 minutes, turning occasionally, until the florets are tender and golden brown in spots (they will continue to brown on the pizza).

PORTOBELLO MUSHROOM PURÉE

Roasting concentrates the flavor of mushrooms, making Portobello Mushroom Purée a wonderfully decadent base for pizza. Don't forget the truffle oil!

MAKES ABOUT 1 CUP

4 portobello mushroom caps, trimmed, gills removed, and sliced

1 tablespoon extra-virgin olive oil

¼ teaspoon chopped fresh thyme leaves

2 cloves chopped Roasted Garlic (see page 36), or ½ teaspoon minced garlic

¼ cup heavy cream

2 teaspoons crème fraîche (or use heavy cream)

Truffle oil

Kosher salt and freshly ground black pepper

1 Preheat the oven to 400°F.

2 Line a sheet pan with parchment paper and set aside.

3 Toss the portobellos with the oil and thyme, then season them with salt and pepper. Evenly spread them in a single layer on the sheet pan and roast them until they are fully cooked, about 20 minutes.

4 Transfer the mushrooms to a medium saucepan. Add the garlic, cream, and crème fraîche. Stir to combine. Bring the mixture to a boil, reduce to a simmer, and cook for about 5 minutes.

5 Strain the mixture through a fine-mesh strainer, reserving the liquid. Transfer the mushroom mixture to a blender and blend, adding just enough of the reserved liquid to make a thick purée. Add truffle oil to taste (start with ½ teaspoon), and, if needed, more salt and pepper.

FIG JAM

Fig Jam is a Figs restaurant classic, and an absolute requirement for Fig and Prosciutto Pizza (see page 127). Don't be tempted to substitute a commercially produced fig jam because it won't have the same savory and sweet flavor profile offered by the stock, wine, and rosemary in this version.

MAKES ABOUT 1 CUP

1 teaspoon canola or vegetable oil

3 shallots, peeled and diced

1 cup red wine

¼ cup chicken broth

¼ cup veal or beef broth

¾ cup balsamic vinegar

1 teaspoon chopped fresh rosemary leaves

¼ cup sugar

1 cup dried mission figs, quartered

1 Place a medium skillet over medium heat and, when it is hot, add the oil. Add the shallots and cook until they are softened, about 3 minutes. Deglaze the pan with the red wine, and cook, stirring occasionally, until the mixture is reduced by half. Stir in the chicken and veal broths and vinegar and cook until the mixture is again reduced by half. Add the rosemary and sugar.

2 Reduce the heat to low and cook until the sugar has dissolved, 3 to 5 minutes. Add the figs and cook, stirring occasionally, until they are rehydrated, 10 to 12 minutes. Continue cooking until the mixture has the consistency of a liquidy jam, another 10 to 12 minutes.

3 Use immediately, or cover and refrigerate for up to 5 days.

WHITE BEAN HUMMUS

Creamy cannellini beans, not chickpeas, are the star of this quick-and-easy hummus. Dollop a few tablespoons on pizzas as soon as they come out of the oven. For a riff on the classic Italian combo of cannellini beans and sage, omit the cumin and paprika and stir in 1 or 2 teaspoons of chopped fresh sage at the end.

MAKES ABOUT 1¼ CUPS

2 cups cooked cannellini beans, or
  1 (15.5-ounce) can cannellini beans, rinsed and drained

3 cloves garlic, chopped

2 tablespoons extra-virgin olive oil

3 tablespoons freshly squeezed lemon juice

½ teaspoon ground cumin, or more to taste

½ teaspoon sweet paprika

1 teaspoon kosher salt (less if using canned beans)

In a food processor, pulse together the beans and garlic until the ingredients are combined. Add the rest of the ingredients and purée until the mixture is smooth, thinning the mixture with water (up to ½ cup) if too thick. Taste, adding more salt or cumin, if needed.

CHICKEN CHILI

Admittedly, it's a bit of effort to make a whole pot of chili as a pizza or flatbread topping, but stay with me here. This chili is delicious on its own, so whether you make it for dinner and use the leftovers for pizza or make it just for the pizza, it's worth it. Plus, if you make it a day in advance and refrigerate it, it tastes even better the next day! Then all you have to do is roll out the dough, add the toppings, and dinner is done in a flash.

MAKES ABOUT 4 CUPS

1 tablespoon vegetable oil

1 pound ground chicken, preferably thigh meat

1½ cups chopped yellow onion

2 tablespoons minced garlic

1 teaspoon red pepper flakes, or to taste

2 tablespoons chili powder

1½ teaspoons ground cumin

2 teaspoons ground coriander

½ teaspoon salt

1 (12-ounce) bottle or can beer

1 (14.5-ounce) can diced tomatoes

2 cups cooked white beans (such as cannellini), or 1 (15.5-ounce) can white beans, rinsed and drained

¼ cup chopped fresh rosemary leaves

¼ cup chopped fresh cilantro leaves

---

1 In a large pot over medium-high heat, heat the oil until hot. Add the chicken, stirring with a wooden spoon to break up any large chunks, until the meat is cooked, about 5 minutes. Add the onions and cook until they are softened, about 5 minutes. Add the garlic, red pepper flakes, chili powder, cumin, coriander, and salt, and cook for 1 minute. Add the beer, tomatoes, and beans, stir well, and bring to a boil.

2 Reduce the heat and simmer, uncovered, for 45 to 60 minutes, stirring occasionally to prevent the chili from sticking to the bottom of the pot.

3 Remove the pot from the heat and add the rosemary and cilantro. Adjust the seasoning, if needed.

ITALIAN MEATBALLS

These meatballs rely on both fresh bread and panko bread crumbs for their tenderness. They're a real treat when sliced in half and placed on a simple pizza with tangy marinara sauce, oozing mozzarella, and a shower of Parmesan. Are you worried about having too many leftover meatballs? I didn't think so.

MAKES ABOUT 3 DOZEN MEATBALLS

1 slice soft white bread, cubed

2 large eggs, lightly beaten

2 tablespoons whole milk

4 teaspoons extra-virgin olive oil

¼ cup chopped yellow onion

2 cloves garlic, chopped

1 pound meatloaf mix (equal parts beef, pork, and veal)

1 teaspoon kosher salt

1 teaspoon freshly ground black pepper

¼ teaspoon red pepper flakes

1½ teaspoons chopped fresh basil

1½ teaspoons chopped fresh thyme

1½ teaspoons chopped fresh oregano

1½ teaspoons chopped fresh parsley

¼ cup freshly grated Parmesan cheese

2 tablespoons tomato sauce

¼ cup panko bread crumbs

1 Preheat the oven to 400°F.

2 In a small bowl, stir together the bread, eggs, and milk. Set aside.

3 In a small skillet, heat 1 teaspoon of the oil until hot and add the onions and garlic and sauté until the onions are translucent, 3 to 4 minutes. Set aside to cool.

4 In a large bowl, loosely combine the remaining ingredients. Stir in the bread and onion mixtures until well combined. Shape into balls about 1 inch in diameter.

5 In a large skillet over medium heat, heat the remaining 1 tablespoon of oil until hot. Working in batches, and being careful not to crowd the pan, add the meatballs in a single layer, turning them during the cooking time until they are browned all over, about 5 minutes. Drain the meatballs on a paper towel-lined plate and repeat with any remaining meatballs.

6 Transfer all the meatballs to a 9 x 13-inch baking dish and bake until they are cooked through, 10 to 15 minutes.

BLACKENED BRUSSELS SPROUTS

Brussels sprouts on pizza? Most definitely yes, especially when combined with cured meats like bacon, prosciutto, pancetta, or salami.

MAKES ½ POUND

2 tablespoons olive oil

2 cloves garlic, thinly sliced

½ pound fresh (not frozen) Brussels sprouts, trimmed and quartered

1 teaspoon freshly squeezed lemon juice

Kosher salt

1 In a large skillet over medium heat, heat the oil until hot. Add the garlic and cook until it is lightly golden brown, being careful not to burn it (or else it will taste bitter). Remove the garlic from the pan and set aside.

2 Increase the heat to medium-high and add the Brussels sprouts. Cook, stirring occasionally, until they are dark brown and caramelized, 8 to 10 minutes; lower the heat to prevent burning if they start to caramelize too quickly.

3 Transfer the Brussels sprouts to a bowl and toss them with the cooked garlic and the lemon juice. Season with salt.

BRUSCHETTA TOMATOES

I chose cherry tomatoes for my Bruschetta Tomatoes because they're reliably sweet, but if you can get your hands on some heirlooms or other beauties from your farmers market, they'd be dynamite here. After all, the quality of a bruschetta rides on the quality of the tomatoes. Be sure to seed your tomatoes or the topping will be too liquidy and could make your pizza soggy.

MAKES ABOUT 1½ CUPS

½ pound cherry tomatoes, seeded and coarsely chopped

1 clove garlic, minced

4 to 5 basil leaves, very thinly sliced

2 to 3 teaspoons extra-virgin olive oil

½ teaspoon balsamic vinegar

Kosher salt and freshly ground black pepper

In a small bowl, stir together the tomatoes, garlic, basil, oil, and vinegar until well combined. Season with salt and pepper.

4

VEGGIE PIZZAS

Rustic pizzas can showcase all the beauty and bounty of the vegetable world—from the simplest recipes, like the famous Margherita (see page 81) or the Pizza Classico (see page 72), to the more inspired, like the Roasted Cauliflower, Mushroom, and Red Onion Pizza (see page 110) or the Fava, Ricotta, Pine Nut, and Pesto Pizza (see page 96). Potatoes, winter and summer squashes, beets, eggplants, greens, and, of course, tomatoes all make their way onto the creative pizzas in this chapter. But don't stop with these: let yourself be inspired by the offerings at your farmers market and see what you can create.

OLIVER PIZZA

Consider the Oliver Pizza your first rustic pizza to master. With savory tomato sauce, beautifully melted mozzarella, and plenty of fresh basil, it's as simple and delicious as it gets—and that's the beauty of it.

2 pizza rounds of your choice

All-purpose flour for sprinkling

2 teaspoons extra-virgin olive oil

½ teaspoon minced garlic

⅔ cup Marinara Sauce (see page 16)

8 ounces mozzarella cheese, shredded

12 whole fresh basil leaves

4 teaspoons freshly grated Parmesan cheese

Kosher salt and freshly ground black pepper

1 One hour before baking, place a baking stone in the oven and preheat it to 500°F (450°F for gluten-free crusts).

2 Roll out 1 pizza round as thinly as possible and place it on a pizza peel sprinkled with flour. Leaving an outer lip all around the edge of the dough, cover the surface with half the oil and garlic; season with salt and pepper.

3 Evenly spread half the sauce on the dough. Top with half each of the mozzarella, basil, and Parmesan.

4 Shake the peel lightly and slide the pizza onto the hot baking stone. Bake until browned, 6 to 7 minutes (10 to 14 minutes for gluten-free crusts).

5 Transfer the pizza to a firm surface and cut it into slices. Serve immediately.

6 Repeat all the steps using the second dough round.

PIZZA BIANCO

Bianco means "white" in Italian, and what makes this pizza *bianco* is the lack of red sauce. If you're a bit skeptical about a no-tomato-sauce pizza, let this one be your "gateway drug." It packs in so much deliciousness from the caramelized onions, mozzarella, balsamic vinegar, and yes, even a few sliced tomatoes for freshness, that you won't miss the marinara.

2 pizza rounds of your choice

All-purpose flour for sprinkling

2 tablespoons plus 2 teaspoons extra-virgin olive oil

½ teaspoon minced garlic

3 cups baby arugula (about 4 ounces)

4 plum tomatoes, sliced and seeded

2 teaspoons balsamic vinegar

6 teaspoons freshly grated Parmesan cheese

8 ounces mozzarella cheese, shredded

⅓ cup Caramelized Onions (see page 38)

Kosher salt and freshly ground black pepper

1 One hour before baking, place a baking stone in the oven and preheat it to 500°F (450°F for gluten-free crusts).

2 Roll out 1 pizza round as thinly as possible and place it on a pizza peel sprinkled with flour. Leaving an outer lip all around the edge of the dough, cover the surface with 1 teaspoon of the oil and half the garlic; season with salt and pepper.

3 Place the arugula, tomatoes, 1 tablespoon oil, vinegar, and 2 teaspoons of the Parmesan in a bowl and toss to combine. Set aside.

4 Evenly sprinkle half the mozzarella on the dough. Top with half the onions and sprinkle with 1 teaspoon of the Parmesan.

5 Shake the peel lightly and slide the pizza onto the hot baking stone. Bake until browned, 6 to 7 minutes (10 to 14 minutes for gluten-free crusts).

6 Transfer the pizza to a firm surface, cover it with half the arugula salad, then cut it into slices. Serve immediately.

7 Repeat all the steps using the second dough round.

WHITE PIZZA

This white pizza variation combines two kinds of garlic, fresh and roasted, with two kinds of cheese, herbed ricotta and mozzarella. You'll want a nice glass of red wine with this one.

2 pizza rounds of your choice

All-purpose flour for sprinkling

2 teaspoons extra-virgin olive oil

1 teaspoon minced garlic

½ head Roasted Garlic (see page 36), cloves peeled and roughly chopped or mashed

½ cup Herbed Ricotta Cheese (see page 41) (or use plain ricotta)

6 ounces mozzarella cheese, shredded

Kosher salt and freshly ground black pepper

1 One hour before baking, place a baking stone in the oven and preheat it to 500°F (450°F for gluten-free crusts).

2 Roll out 1 pizza round as thinly as possible and place it on a pizza peel sprinkled with flour. Leaving an outer lip all around the edge of the dough, cover the surface with half the oil and half each of the minced and roasted garlics; season with salt and pepper.

3 Evenly spread half the ricotta on top, then top with half the mozzarella.

4 Shake the peel lightly and slide the pizza onto the hot baking stone. Bake until browned, 6 to 7 minutes (10 to 14 minutes for gluten-free crusts).

5 Transfer the pizza to a firm surface and cut into slices. Serve immediately.

6 Repeat all the steps using the second dough round.

WHITE BEAN HUMMUS AND ASIAGO PIZZA

Topped with creamy white bean hummus, sweet caramelized onions, rich Asiago cheese, and peppery arugula, this pizza is elegant and surprisingly light.

2 pizza rounds of your choice

All-purpose flour for sprinkling

2 teaspoons extra-virgin olive oil

½ teaspoon minced garlic

½ cup freshly grated Asiago cheese

½ cup Caramelized Onions (see page 38)

2 tablespoons freshly grated Parmesan cheese

1½ cups baby arugula (about 2 ounces)

3 tablespoons White Bean Hummus (see page 59)

Kosher salt and freshly ground black pepper

1 One hour before baking, place a baking stone in the oven and preheat it to 500°F (450°F for gluten-free crusts).

2 Roll out 1 pizza round as thinly as possible and place it on a pizza peel sprinkled with flour. Leaving an outer lip all around the edge of the dough, cover the surface with half the oil and garlic; season with salt and pepper.

3 Evenly distribute half each of the Asiago, onions, and Parmesan on the dough.

4 Shake the peel lightly and slide the pizza onto the hot baking stone. Bake until browned, 6 to 7 minutes (10 to 14 minutes for gluten-free crusts).

5 Transfer the pizza to a firm surface, top with half the arugula, then drizzle with half the hummus. Cut the pizza into slices and serve immediately.

6 Repeat all the steps using the second dough round.

PIZZA CLASSICO

There's nowhere to hide an inferior crust here, because Pizza Classico is barely dressed—just a little tomato sauce, a swirl of basil oil, and a few shavings of Parmesan.

2 pizza rounds of your choice

All-purpose flour for sprinkling

2 tablespoons Basil Oil (see page 28)

4 tablespoons Marinara Sauce (see page 16)

2 tablespoons freshly shaved Parmesan cheese

Kosher salt and freshly ground black pepper

1 One hour before baking, place a baking stone in the oven and preheat it to 500°F (450°F for gluten-free crusts).

2 Roll out 1 pizza round as thinly as possible and place it on a pizza peel sprinkled with flour. Leaving an outer lip all around the edge of the dough, season the surface with salt and pepper.

3 Add half the basil oil and half the sauce on the dough and spread them together with a spoon; it will form a thin cover on the surface.

4 Shake the peel lightly and slide the pizza onto the hot baking stone. Bake until browned, 6 to 7 minutes (10 to 14 minutes for gluten-free crusts).

5 Transfer the pizza to a firm surface, sprinkle it with half the Parmesan, then cut it into slices and serve immediately.

6 Repeat all the steps using the second dough round.

POTATO, ALMOND PESTO, AND FONTINA PIZZA

Potatoes on pizza might seem unusual at first, but once you have a taste of this potato, almond pesto, and Fontina pizza you'll realize how natural the combination is. In fact, according to Italian food legend and cookbook author Marcella Hazan, in Genoa, spaghetti with pesto sauce is often served with new potatoes. It's a (carbohydrate-rich) match made in heaven. Here delicious Fontina rounds out the pie.

2 pizza rounds of your choice

All-purpose flour for sprinkling

2 teaspoons extra-virgin olive oil

½ teaspoon minced garlic

½ cup Almond Pesto (see page 21)

4 ounces Fontina cheese, thinly sliced

4 boiled or roasted new potatoes, each sliced into 4 to 5 rounds

2 teaspoons freshly grated Parmesan cheese

2 tablespoons toasted slivered almonds, for garnish

Kosher salt and freshly ground black pepper

1 One hour before baking, place a baking stone in the oven and preheat it to 500°F (450°F for gluten-free crusts).

2 Roll out 1 pizza round as thinly as possible and place it on a pizza peel sprinkled with flour. Leaving an outer lip all around the edge of the dough, cover the surface with half the oil and garlic; season with salt and pepper.

3 Evenly spread half the pesto on the dough. Top with half each of the Fontina and sliced potatoes. Sprinkle with half the Parmesan.

4 Shake the peel lightly and slide the pizza onto the hot baking stone. Bake until browned, 6 to 7 minutes (10 to 14 minutes for gluten-free crusts).

5 Transfer the pizza to a firm surface and cut it into slices. Serve immediately, topped with half the slivered almonds.

6 Repeat all the steps using the second dough round.

SPICY SPINACH AND FETA PIZZA

The inspiration for Spicy Spinach, Tomato, and Feta Pizza comes from spanakopita, a Greek spinach and onion pie made with feta and layers of phyllo dough. This pizza is packed with its own layers of bold flavors, from the roasted onions and the oregano-infused tomatoes to the briny feta cheese and spicy spinach leaves. For another Greek-inspired pizza, try Greek-Style Pizza (see page 201).

4 plum tomatoes, quartered and seeded

1 tablespoon fresh oregano leaves

1 tablespoon plus 2 teaspoons extra-virgin olive oil

⅛ teaspoon freshly ground black pepper

2 pizza rounds of your choice

All-purpose flour for sprinkling

½ teaspoon minced garlic

½ cup Sautéed Spicy Spinach (see page 50), chopped

2 tablespoons Roasted Red Onions (see page 37)

4 tablespoons (2 ounces) feta cheese, crumbled

1 teaspoon freshly grated Parmesan cheese

Kosher salt and freshly ground black pepper

1 One hour before baking, place a baking stone in the oven and preheat it to 500°F (450°F for gluten-free crusts).

2 In a small bowl, toss together the tomatoes, oregano, 1 tablespoon of the oil, and the pepper. Set aside.

3 Roll out 1 pizza round as thinly as possible and place it on a pizza peel sprinkled with flour. Leaving an outer lip all around the edge of the dough, cover the surface with 1 teaspoon of the oil and half the garlic; season with salt and pepper.

4 Evenly distribute half the spicy spinach on the dough. Top with half each of the tomatoes, roasted onions, feta, and Parmesan.

5 Shake the peel lightly and slide the pizza onto the hot baking stone. Bake until browned, 6 to 7 minutes (10 to 14 minutes for gluten-free crusts).

6 Transfer the pizza to a firm surface and cut it into slices. Serve immediately.

7 Repeat all the steps (except step 2) using the second dough round.

PORTOBELLO AND FONTINA PIZZA

Double up on the mushroom goodness with portobello mushrooms, mushroom purée, and Fontina pizza, which combines two incredible textures on one pizza: a delicious roasted, truffle-flavored mushroom purée with fresh sliced portobellos. Don't forget the additional truffle oil drizzle at the end!

2 pizza rounds of your choice

All-purpose flour for sprinkling

2 teaspoons extra-virgin olive oil

½ teaspoon minced garlic

6 ounces Fontina cheese, shredded

1 cup Portobello Mushroom Purée (see page 56)

2 portobello mushroom caps, trimmed and thinly sliced on an angle

2 tablespoons freshly grated Parmesan cheese

Truffle oil, for garnish (optional)

Kosher salt and freshly ground black pepper

1 One hour before baking, place a baking stone in the oven and preheat it to 500°F (450°F for gluten-free crusts).

2 Roll out 1 pizza round as thinly as possible and place it on a pizza peel sprinkled with flour. Leaving an outer lip all around the edge of the dough, cover the surface with half the oil and garlic; season with salt and pepper.

3 Evenly distribute half the Fontina on the dough. Top with half each of the mushroom purée and the portobello slices. Sprinkle with 1½ teaspoons of the Parmesan.

4 Shake the peel lightly and slide the pizza onto the hot baking stone. Bake until browned, 6 to 7 minutes (10 to 14 minutes for gluten-free crusts).

5 Transfer the pizza to a firm surface and cut it into slices. Serve immediately, garnished with 1½ teaspoons Parmesan, a pinch of pepper, and a tiny drizzle of truffle oil, if desired.

6 Repeat all the steps using the second dough round.

ASPARAGUS AND MUSHROOM PURÉE PIZZA

Asparagus and mushrooms are so perfect together. Use the freshest in-season asparagus you can find, preferably straight from your favorite farmers market stall.

2 pizza rounds of your choice

All-purpose flour for sprinkling

2 teaspoons extra-virgin olive oil

½ teaspoon minced garlic

Kosher salt and freshly ground black pepper

6 ounces Fontina cheese, shredded

1 cup Portobello Mushroom Purée (see page 56)

12 asparagus spears, peeled and halved lengthwise

2 teaspoons freshly grated Parmesan cheese

1 One hour before baking, place a baking stone in the oven and preheat it to 500°F (450°F for gluten-free crusts).

2 Roll out 1 pizza round as thinly as possible and place it on a pizza peel sprinkled with flour. Leaving an outer lip all around the edge of the dough, cover the surface with half the oil and garlic; season with salt and pepper.

3 Evenly sprinkle half the Fontina on the dough. Top with half each of the mushroom purée and asparagus spears, then sprinkle with ½ teaspoon of the Parmesan.

4 Shake the peel lightly and slide the pizza onto the hot baking stone. Bake until browned, 6 to 7 minutes (10 to 14 minutes for gluten-free crusts).

5 Transfer the pizza to a firm surface and cut it into slices. Serve immediately, garnished with ½ teaspoon of the Parmesan.

6 Repeat all the steps using the second dough round.

WILD MUSHROOM PIZZA

Wild mushrooms were made for pizza! You can try a combination of a few different kinds, such as chanterelle, shiitake, and oyster, or just use a single variety if that's all you can find. To prepare the mushrooms, follow the method for the Sautéed Mushrooms (see page 49). A half pound of raw mushrooms will cook down to about 1 cup.

2 cups baby arugula (about 2½ ounces)

2 teaspoons freshly squeezed lemon juice

2 tablespoons extra-virgin olive oil

2 pizza rounds of your choice

All-purpose flour for sprinkling

1 cup Portobello Mushroom Purée (see page 56)

8 ounces wild mushrooms, sautéed (see headnote)

3 ounces fresh mozzarella cheese, thinly sliced

3 ounces Fontina cheese, thinly sliced

½ teaspoon chopped fresh marjoram, or ⅛ teaspoon dried marjoram

2 tablespoons freshly grated Parmesan cheese

Kosher salt and freshly ground black pepper

1 One hour before baking, place a baking stone in the oven and preheat it to 500°F (450°F for gluten-free crusts).

2 In a small bowl, toss 1 cup of the arugula with half the lemon juice and oil. Set aside.

3 Roll out 1 pizza round as thinly as possible and place it on a pizza peel sprinkled with flour. Leaving an outer lip all around the edge of the dough, season the surface with salt and pepper.

4 Evenly spread half the mushroom purée on the dough. Top with half each of the wild mushrooms, mozzarella, Fontina, and marjoram. Top with ½ cup of the arugula salad and half the Parmesan.

5 Shake the peel lightly and slide the pizza onto the hot baking stone. Bake until browned 6 to 7 minutes (10 to 14 minutes for gluten-free crusts).

6 Transfer the pizza to a firm surface, garnish it with the remaining arugula salad, and cut it into slices. Serve immediately.

7 Repeat all the steps using the second dough round.

MUSHROOM PURÉE AND HERBED GOAT CHEESE PIZZA

Rich, roasted portobello mushroom purée meets tangy herbed goat cheese. Drizzle the finished pizza with balsamic vinegar for a little sweetness to pull all the flavors together.

2 pizza rounds of your choice

All-purpose flour for sprinkling

2 teaspoons extra-virgin olive oil

½ teaspoon minced garlic

1 cup Portobello Mushroom Purée (see page 56)

½ cup Herbed Goat Cheese (see page 41)

2 teaspoons freshly grated Parmesan cheese

1 tablespoon balsamic vinegar, for garnish (optional)

Kosher salt and freshly ground black pepper

1 One hour before baking, place a baking stone in the oven and preheat it to 500°F (450°F for gluten-free crusts).

2 Roll out 1 pizza round as thinly as possible and place it on a pizza peel sprinkled with flour. Leaving an outer lip all around the edge of the dough, cover the surface with half the oil and garlic; season with salt and pepper.

3 Evenly spread half the mushroom purée on the dough and dot with half the herbed goat cheese. Sprinkle with half the Parmesan.

4 Shake the peel lightly and slide the pizza onto the hot baking stone. Bake until browned, 6 to 7 minutes (10 to 14 minutes for gluten-free crusts).

5 Transfer the pizza to a firm surface and it cut into slices. Serve immediately, garnished with half the balsamic vinegar, if desired.

6 Repeat all the steps using the second dough round.

MARGHERITA

Legend has it that the iconic Margherita pizza is red, green, and white to match the colors of the Italian flag. (Red for tomato, green for basil, and white for mozzarella, of course.) Regardless of whether or not that's true, the Margherita is one of the most traditional pizzas you can make. My version uses basil oil for more concentrated basil flavor (consider it the secret ingredient). Be extra careful to maintain the outer lip on the crust; you don't want the oil to slide off and burn.

2 pizza rounds of your choice

All-purpose flour for sprinkling

½ teaspoon minced garlic

¼ cup Basil Oil (see page 28)

6 ounces fresh mozzarella cheese, thinly sliced

2 plum tomatoes, sliced and seeded

2 tablespoons freshly grated Parmesan cheese

2 tablespoons chopped fresh basil or parsley leaves, for garnish

Kosher salt and freshly ground black pepper

1 One hour before baking, place a baking stone in the oven and preheat it to 500°F (450°F for gluten-free crusts).

2 Roll out 1 pizza round as thinly as possible and place it on a pizza peel sprinkled with flour. Leaving an outer lip all around the edge of the dough, sprinkle with half the garlic and season with salt and pepper.

3 Evenly spread half the basil oil on the dough. Top with half each of the mozzarella and tomatoes and 1½ teaspoons of the Parmesan.

4 Shake the peel lightly and slide the pizza onto the hot baking stone. Bake until browned, 6 to 7 minutes (10 to 14 minutes for gluten-free crusts).

5 Transfer the pizza to a firm surface and cut it into slices. Serve immediately, garnished with 1½ teaspoons of the Parmesan and half the basil.

6 Repeat all the steps using the second dough round.

LEEK, POTATO, AND GRUYÈRE PIZZA

Leeks and potatoes are a classic and comforting combination—think leek and potato soup! Here the leeks are caramelized until they're sweet and delicious. The mustard aioli adds a bright note of contrast, but a little smear of plain Dijon works too!

2 pizza rounds of your choice

All-purpose flour for sprinkling

1½ tablespoon unsalted butter

2 teaspoons extra-virgin olive oil

½ teaspoon minced garlic

5-6 leeks, washed and julienned

4 boiled or roasted new potatoes, each sliced into 4 to 5 rounds

4 ounces Gruyère cheese, shredded

2 teaspoons freshly grated Parmesan cheese

1 teaspoon fresh thyme leaves

½ teaspoon chopped fresh rosemary leaves

Mustard Aioli (see page 34) or Dijon mustard, for garnish (optional)

Kosher salt and freshly ground black pepper

1 One hour before baking, place a baking stone in the oven and preheat it to 500°F (450°F for gluten-free crusts).

2 Place the butter and oil in a large skillet over medium heat. When the butter has melted, reduce heat to low, add the leeks, and stir. Cook, stirring regularly, until they are lightly browned, about 30 minutes.

3 Roll out 1 pizza round as thinly as possible and place it on a pizza peel sprinkled with flour. Leaving an outer lip all around the edge of the dough, cover the surface with 1 tablespoon oil and half the garlic; season with salt and pepper.

4 Evenly distribute half the caramelized leeks on the dough. Top with half each of the sliced potatoes, Gruyère, and Parmesan. Sprinkle with half the thyme and rosemary.

5 Shake the peel lightly and slide the pizza onto the hot baking stone. Bake until browned, 6 to 7 minutes (10 to 14 minutes for gluten-free crusts).

6 Transfer the pizza to a firm surface and cut it into slices. Serve immediately, lightly drizzled with the mustard aioli, if desired.

7 Repeat all the steps (except step 2) using the second dough round.

GOLDEN BEET AND WALNUT GORGONZOLA PIZZA

Beets are like brilliant gems, and this pizza looks like a golden ray of sunshine. Feel free to substitute red beets if that's all you can find at the supermarket, but your local farmers market might also have the golden ones when in season.

2 pizza rounds of your choice

All-purpose flour for sprinkling

2 teaspoons extra-virgin olive oil

½ teaspoon minced garlic

4 ounces mozzarella cheese, shredded

1 Roasted Golden Beet (see page 43), peeled and very thinly sliced

¼ cup Walnut Gorgonzola (see page 44)

2 tablespoons freshly grated Pecorino Romano cheese

Fresh arugula or basil leaves, for garnish (optional)

Balsamic vinegar, for garnish (optional)

Kosher salt and freshly ground black pepper

1 One hour before baking, place a baking stone in the oven and preheat it to 500°F (450°F for gluten-free crusts).

2 Roll out 1 pizza round as thinly as possible and place it on a pizza peel sprinkled with flour. Leaving an outer lip all around the edge of the dough, cover the surface with half the oil and garlic; season with salt and pepper.

3 Evenly sprinkle half the mozzarella over the dough. Top with half the beet, dot with half the walnut Gorgonzola, and sprinkle with half the Pecorino Romano.

4 Shake the peel lightly and slide the pizza onto the hot baking stone. Bake until browned, 6 to 7 minutes (10 to 14 minutes for gluten-free crusts).

5 Transfer the pizza to a firm surface and cut it into slices. Serve immediately, garnished with a few arugula leaves and a drizzle of balsamic vinegar, if desired.

6 Repeat all the steps using the second dough round.

BUTTERNUT SQUASH AND SAGE WITH ROASTED GARLIC BÉCHAMEL PIZZA

You might not have thought of using butternut squash on pizza, but this sweet, nutty, and versatile winter squash is good for much more than just soup and ravioli. Here it combines with creamy garlic béchamel and woodsy sage for a savory, hearty take on pizza that's perfect for a cold winter's night.

2 pizza rounds of your choice

All-purpose flour for sprinkling

2 teaspoons extra-virgin olive oil

½ teaspoon minced garlic

½ cup Roasted Garlic Béchamel (see page 25)

4 ounces mozzarella cheese, shredded

1½ cups Roasted Butternut Squash (see page 39)

8 large sage leaves

2 tablespoons freshly grated Parmesan cheese

Kosher salt and freshly ground black pepper

1 One hour before baking, place a baking stone in the oven and preheat it to 500°F (450°F for gluten-free crusts).

2 Roll out 1 pizza round as thinly as possible and place it on a pizza peel sprinkled with flour. Leaving an outer lip all around the edge of the dough, cover the surface with half the oil and garlic; season with salt and pepper.

3 Evenly spread half the béchamel over the dough. Top with half each of the mozzarella, squash, and sage. Sprinkle with half the Parmesan.

4 Shake the peel lightly and slide the pizza onto the hot baking stone. Bake until browned, 6 to 7 minutes (10 to 14 minutes for gluten-free crusts).

5 Transfer the pizza to a firm surface and cut it into slices. Serve immediately.

6 Repeat all the steps using the second dough round.

ROASTED EGGPLANT PIZZA

This isn't exactly eggplant parmesan on a pizza—for something a bit closer see the Crispy Eggplant Pizza on page 46. To start, the eggplant here is roasted until meltingly tender, not breaded and fried. That said, if you love eggplant parmesan, this pizza—with its generous dollops of ricotta—should be right up your alley. For a more elegant look, thinly slice the eggplant lengthwise before roasting it, then fan the slices out on the pizza. Since eggplants come in different sizes, I've just specified that you use one eggplant, but you may not need all of it.

2 pizza rounds of your choice

All-purpose flour for sprinkling

2 teaspoons extra-virgin olive oil

½ teaspoon minced garlic

⅔ cup Marinara Sauce (see page 16)

6 ounces fresh mozzarella cheese, thinly sliced

1 Roasted Eggplant (see page 45), thinly sliced (any extra saved for another use)

2 tablespoons freshly grated Parmesan cheese

⅓ cup ricotta cheese

2 tablespoons sliced fresh basil, for garnish

Kosher salt and freshly ground black pepper

1 One hour before baking, place a baking stone in the oven and preheat it to 500°F (450°F for gluten-free crusts).

2 Roll out 1 pizza round as thinly as possible and place it on a pizza peel sprinkled with flour. Leaving an outer lip all around the edge of the dough, cover the surface with half the oil and garlic; season with salt and pepper.

3 Evenly spread half the sauce on the dough. Top with half each of the mozzarella and the eggplant slices. Sprinkle with half the Parmesan. Dot with half the ricotta.

4 Shake the peel lightly and slide the pizza onto the hot baking stone. Bake until browned, 6 to 7 minutes (10 to 14 minutes for gluten-free crusts).

5 Transfer the pizza to a firm surface and it cut into slices. Serve immediately, garnished with half the basil.

6 Repeat all the steps using the second dough round.

TRIPLE-THREAT ROASTED EGGPLANT, TOMATO, AND ONION PIZZA

This delicious pizza takes advantage of all of the deep flavors that roasting produces. Don't leave out the basil—it provides a fresh note of contrast.

2 pizza rounds of your choice

All-purpose flour for sprinkling

2 teaspoons extra-virgin olive oil

½ teaspoon minced garlic

⅔ cup Roasted Tomato Sauce (see page 17)

6 ounces mozzarella cheese, shredded

1 Roasted Eggplant (see page 45), thinly sliced (any extra saved for another use)

½ cup Roasted Red Onions (see page 37)

2 tablespoons freshly grated Parmesan cheese

2 tablespoons chopped fresh basil leaves, for garnish

Kosher salt and freshly ground black pepper

1 One hour before baking, place a baking stone in the oven and preheat it to 500°F (450°F for gluten-free crusts).

2 Roll out 1 pizza round as thinly as possible and place it on a pizza peel sprinkled with flour. Leaving an outer lip all around the edge of the dough, cover the surface with half the oil and garlic; season with salt and pepper.

3 Evenly spread half the sauce on the dough. Top with half each of the mozzarella, eggplant slices, and onions. Sprinkle with half the Parmesan.

4 Shake the peel lightly and slide the pizza onto the hot baking stone. Bake until browned, 6 to 7 minutes (10 to 14 minutes for gluten-free crusts).

5 Transfer the pizza to a firm surface and cut it into slices. Serve immediately, garnished with half the basil.

6 Repeat all the steps using the second dough round.

BRUSCHETTA PIZZA

A classic Italian appetizer, bruschetta is grilled or toasted bread that's been rubbed with garlic and olive oil and then topped with tomatoes. Bruschetta is also the platform for homey and soul-satisfying pizza. Here I use my bruschetta tomatoes, which are seasoned with fresh basil and sweet balsamic vinegar, to top a garlicky, cheesy crust.

2 pizza rounds of your choice

All-purpose flour for sprinkling

2 teaspoons extra-virgin olive oil

1 teaspoon minced garlic

3 ounces mozzarella cheese, shredded

3 ounces Fontina cheese, shredded (or use mozzarella)

2 tablespoons freshly grated Parmesan cheese

1½ cups Bruschetta Tomatoes (see page 64)

Kosher salt and freshly ground black pepper

1 One hour before baking, place a baking stone in the oven and preheat it to 500°F (450°F for gluten-free crusts).

2 Roll out 1 pizza round as thinly as possible and place it on a pizza peel sprinkled with flour. Leaving an outer lip all around the edge of the dough, cover the surface with half the oil and garlic; season with salt and pepper.

3 Evenly spread half the cheeses on the dough.

4 Shake the peel lightly and slide the pizza onto the hot baking stone. Bake until browned, 6 to 7 minutes (10 to 14 minutes for gluten-free crusts).

5 Transfer the pizza to a firm surface, top it with half the tomatoes, and cut it into slices. Serve immediately.

6 Repeat all the steps using the second dough round.

ROASTED EGGPLANT AND BALSAMIC ONIONS PIZZA

Meaty roasted eggplant and sweet and savory balsamic onions echo some of the flavors of an *agrodolce caponata* (a sweet-and-sour Sicilian dish usually served as a salad). If you like capers, add a few to each pizza along with the eggplant.

2 pizza rounds of your choice

All-purpose flour for sprinkling

2 teaspoons extra-virgin olive oil

½ teaspoon minced garlic

½ cup Balsamic Onions (see page 37)

6 ounces mozzarella cheese, shredded

1 Roasted Eggplant (see page 45), thinly sliced (any extra saved for another use)

4 teaspoons freshly grated Parmesan cheese

Handful fresh basil leaves, torn, for garnish

Kosher salt and freshly ground black pepper

1 One hour before baking, place a baking stone in the oven and preheat it to 500°F (450°F for gluten-free crusts).

2 Roll out 1 pizza round as thinly as possible and place it on a pizza peel sprinkled with flour. Leaving an outer lip all around the edge of the dough, cover the surface with half the oil and garlic; season with salt and pepper.

3 Evenly distribute half the onions on the dough. Top with half each of the mozzarella and the eggplant slices. Sprinkle with half the Parmesan.

4 Shake the peel lightly and slide the pizza onto the hot baking stone. Bake until browned, 6 to 7 minutes (10 to 14 minutes for gluten-free crusts).

5 Transfer the pizza to a firm surface and cut it into slices. Serve immediately, garnished with half the basil.

6 Repeat all the steps using the second dough round.

CRISPY EGGPLANT PIZZA

If you like eggplant parmesan, put Crispy Eggplant Pizza on the top of your to-make list, as it hits all the right flavor and texture notes—crunchy, gooey, chewy, and utterly delicious. The secret is the super-thin eggplant slices that maximize the crispiness factor.

2 pizza rounds of your choice

All-purpose flour for sprinkling

2 teaspoons extra-virgin olive oil

½ teaspoon minced garlic

1 cup Marinara Sauce (see page 16)

8 ounces mozzarella cheese, shredded

2 plum tomatoes, thinly sliced and seeded

1 Crispy Eggplant (see page 46)

½ cup Herbed Ricotta Cheese (see page 41) (or use plain ricotta)

16 fresh basil leaves

2 tablespoons freshly grated Parmesan cheese

Kosher salt and freshly ground black pepper

1 One hour before baking, place a baking stone in the oven and preheat it to 500°F (450°F for gluten-free crusts).

2 Roll out 1 pizza round as thinly as possible and place it on a pizza peel sprinkled with flour. Leaving an outer lip all around the edge of the dough, cover the surface with half the oil and garlic; season with salt and pepper.

3 Evenly spread half each of the sauce, mozzarella, tomatoes, and eggplant on the dough. Dot with half the ricotta and top with half the basil. Sprinkle with half the Parmesan.

4 Shake the peel lightly and slide the pizza onto the hot baking stone. Bake until browned, 6 to 7 minutes (10 to 14 minutes for gluten-free crusts).

5 Transfer the pizza to a firm surface and cut it into slices. Serve immediately.

6 Repeat all the steps using the second dough round.

ZUCCHINI, ONION, AND RICOTTA PIZZA

If you're a home gardener, then Zucchini, Onion, and Ricotta Pizza is a great way of using up some of your extra squash. If you don't have the caramelized onions handy, don't let that stop you. Just add raw slices of whatever kind of onion you have around after you add the cheese—a sweet onion like Vidalia would be tops.

2 pizza rounds of your choice

All-purpose flour for sprinkling

2 teaspoons extra-virgin olive oil

½ teaspoon minced garlic

⅔ cup Fresh Tomato Sauce (see page 20)

6 ounces mozzarella cheese, shredded

1 Grilled Zucchini (see page 47)

½ cup Caramelized Onions (see page 38)

⅓ cup ricotta cheese

2 tablespoons freshly grated Pecorino Romano or Parmesan cheese

2 tablespoons thinly sliced fresh basil, for garnish

Kosher salt and freshly ground black pepper

1 One hour before baking, place a baking stone in the oven and preheat it to 500°F (450°F for gluten-free crusts).

2 Roll out 1 pizza round as thinly as possible and place it on a pizza peel sprinkled with flour. Leaving an outer lip all around the edge of the dough, cover the surface with half the oil and garlic; season with salt and pepper.

3 Evenly spread half the sauce on the dough. Top with half each of the mozzarella, zucchini, and onions. Dot with half the ricotta and sprinkle with half the Pecorino Romano.

4 Shake the peel lightly and slide the pizza onto the hot baking stone. Bake until browned, 6 to 7 minutes (10 to 14 minutes for gluten-free crusts).

5 Transfer the pizza to a firm surface and cut it into slices. Serve immediately, garnished with half the basil.

6 Repeat all the steps using the second dough round.

FRESH TOMATO, BRAISED FENNEL, AND GORGONZOLA PIZZA

Fennel's licoricey notes may not be to everyone's taste, but I think it's great shaved on salads and in other raw preparations, including pizza. If you don't like it raw, give braising a try—it softens and mellows the fennel and coaxes out even more of its natural sweetness. Here, it's contrasted with tangy Gorgonzola and fresh tomato.

2 pizza rounds of your choice

All-purpose flour for sprinkling

2 teaspoons extra-virgin olive oil

½ teaspoon minced garlic

6 ounces mozzarella cheese, shredded

½ cup Braised Fennel (see page 40), well drained

4 plum tomatoes, cut into ¼-inch rounds and seeded

2 ounces Gorgonzola cheese, crumbled

Kosher salt and freshly ground black pepper

1 One hour before baking, place a baking stone in the oven and preheat it to 500°F (450°F for gluten-free crusts).

2 Roll out 1 pizza round as thinly as possible and place it on a pizza peel sprinkled with flour. Leaving an outer lip all around the edge of the dough, cover the surface with half the oil and garlic; season with salt and pepper.

3 Evenly sprinkle half the mozzarella on the dough. Top with half each of the fennel and tomatoes and dot with half the Gorgonzola.

4 Shake the peel lightly and slide the pizza onto the hot baking stone. Bake until browned, 6 to 7 minutes (10 to 14 minutes for gluten-free crusts).

5 Transfer the pizza to a firm surface and cut it into slices. Serve immediately.

6 Repeat all the steps using the second dough round.

SHIITAKE AND ROASTED GARLIC BÉCHAMEL PIZZA

Simple and delicious, this pizza combines the richness of shiitake mushrooms with creamy béchamel and Fontina. If you've got leftover roasted garlic after making the béchamel, use a few cloves on the pizza as a topping.

2 pizza rounds of your choice

All-purpose flour for sprinkling

½ teaspoon minced garlic

½ cup Roasted Garlic Béchamel (see page 25)

4 ounces Fontina cheese, shredded

4 ounces shiitake mushrooms, stems removed and discarded, tops thinly sliced

¼ red onion, peeled and thinly sliced

Kosher salt and freshly ground black pepper

1 One hour before baking, place a baking stone in the oven and preheat it to 500°F (450°F for gluten-free crusts).

2 Roll out 1 pizza round as thinly as possible and place it on a pizza peel sprinkled with flour. Leaving an outer lip all around the edge of the dough, cover the surface with half the garlic; season with salt and pepper.

3 Evenly spread half the béchamel on the dough. Top with half each of the Fontina, mushrooms, and onion.

4 Shake the peel lightly and slide the pizza onto the hot baking stone. Bake until browned, 6 to 7 minutes (10 to 14 minutes for gluten-free crusts).

5 Transfer the pizza to a firm surface and cut it into slices. Serve immediately.

6 Repeat all the steps using the second dough round.

FAVA, RICOTTA, PINE NUT, AND PESTO PIZZA

Fresh fava beans, which are in season in spring, are a deliciously buttery and nutty addition to pizza. It's true that they're a bit of work: you have to take them out of their pods, blanch the beans, then peel each bean individually. But once you taste them, you'll realize it was worth all the effort. The ricotta and pesto work together to boost the fresh taste. Don't substitute dried favas here; the flavor won't be the same. Now, if you could *also* happen to get your hands on some fresh morels (and sauté them gently in butter), I'm just saying they wouldn't be bad here.

2 pizza rounds of your choice

All-purpose flour for sprinkling

⅓ cup Traditional Basil Pesto (see page 23)

4 ounces fresh mozzarella, shredded

½ cup ricotta cheese

¾ to 1 cup blanched and peeled fresh fava beans

1 to 2 tablespoons pine nuts

2 tablespoons sliced fresh basil leaves, for garnish

Kosher salt and freshly ground black pepper

1 One hour before baking, place a baking stone in the oven and preheat it to 500°F (450°F for gluten-free crusts).

2 Roll out 1 pizza round as thinly as possible and place it on a pizza peel sprinkled with flour. Leaving an outer lip all around the edge of the dough, season the surface with salt and pepper.

3 Evenly spread half the pesto on the dough and top with half the mozzarella. Dot with half the ricotta and scatter half the fava beans and pine nuts on top.

4 Shake the peel lightly and slide the pizza onto the hot baking stone. Bake until browned, 6 to 7 minutes (10 to 14 minutes for gluten-free crusts).

5 Transfer the pizza to a firm surface and cut it into slices. Serve immediately, garnished with half the basil.

6 Repeat all the steps using the second dough round.

QUATTRO FORMAGGIO PIZZA

Quattro formaggio means "four cheeses" in Italian, and that's exactly what you'll get here—delicate mozzarella, melty Fontina, sharp Provolone, and creamy ricotta. Fresh tomato sauce keeps it from being too heavy, but if you're all about the cheese, you can even leave it out.

2 pizza rounds of your choice

All-purpose flour for sprinkling

2 teaspoons extra-virgin olive oil

½ teaspoon minced garlic

2 ounces mozzarella cheese, shredded

2 ounces Fontina cheese, shredded

2 ounces Provolone cheese, shredded

⅔ cup Fresh Tomato Sauce (see page 20)

2 ounces ricotta cheese

12 whole fresh basil leaves

Kosher salt and freshly ground
  black pepper

1 One hour before baking, place a baking stone in the oven and preheat it to 500°F (450°F for gluten-free crusts).

2 Roll out 1 pizza round as thinly as possible and place it on a pizza peel sprinkled with flour. Leaving an outer lip all around the edge of the dough, cover the surface with half the oil and garlic; season with salt and pepper.

3 In a small bowl, stir together the mozzarella, Fontina, and Provolone cheeses until evenly combined.

4 Evenly spread half the sauce on the dough. Top with half the cheese mixture, dollop with half the ricotta, and top with half the basil.

5 Shake the peel lightly and slide the pizza onto the hot baking stone. Bake until browned, 6 to 7 minutes (10 to 14 minutes for gluten-free crusts).

6 Transfer the pizza to a firm surface and cut it into slices. Serve immediately.

7 Repeat all the steps (except step 3) using the second dough round.

MARINATED ARTICHOKE HEARTS WITH HERBED GOAT CHEESE AND SHAVED PARMESAN PIZZA

A popular hors d'oeuvre, marinated artichoke hearts add zest and texture to a pizza. It's perfectly fine to use artichokes from a jar here. They're delicious with the tangy herbed goat cheese and the nutty Parmesan.

2 pizza rounds of your choice

All-purpose flour for sprinkling

2 teaspoons extra-virgin olive oil

½ teaspoon minced garlic

½ cup Caramelized Onions (see page 38)

3 to 4 marinated artichoke hearts, sliced

½ cup Herbed Goat Cheese (see page 41)

1 ounce Parmesan cheese, shaved

Kosher salt and freshly ground black pepper

1 One hour before baking, place a baking stone in the oven and preheat it to 500°F (450°F for gluten-free crusts).

2 Roll out 1 pizza round as thinly as possible and place it on a pizza peel sprinkled with flour. Leaving an outer lip all around the edge of the dough, cover the surface with half the oil and garlic; season with salt and pepper.

3 Evenly distribute half the onions on the dough. Top with half the artichoke slices, and dot with half the herbed goat cheese and Parmesan.

4 Shake the peel lightly and slide the pizza onto the hot baking stone. Bake until browned, 6 to 7 minutes (10 to 14 minutes for gluten-free crusts).

5 Transfer the pizza to a firm surface and cut it into slices. Serve immediately.

6 Repeat all the steps using the second dough round.

ROASTED PEAR, CAMEMBERT, AND WATERCRESS PIZZA

Pear and blue cheese are an incredible flavor combination that is great for salads, but even better on pizza.

2 pizza rounds of your choice

All-purpose flour for sprinkling

2 teaspoons extra-virgin olive oil

1 Roasted Pear (see page 48), thinly sliced

6 ounces Camembert cheese

2 cups watercress leaves

Balsamic vinegar, for garnish

Kosher salt and freshly ground black pepper

1 One hour before baking, place a baking stone in the oven and preheat it to 500°F (450°F for gluten-free crusts).

2 Roll out 1 pizza round as thinly as possible and place it on a pizza peel sprinkled with flour. Leaving an outer lip all around the edge of the dough, cover the surface with half the oil; season with salt and pepper.

3 Evenly distribute half the pear on the dough and dot with half the Camembert.

4 Shake the peel lightly and slide the pizza onto the hot baking stone. Bake until browned, 6 to 7 minutes (10 to 14 minutes for gluten-free crusts).

5 Transfer the pizza to a firm surface and it cut into slices. Serve immediately, topped with half the watercress and a drizzle of balsamic vinegar.

6 Repeat all the steps using the second dough round.

PEAR, GORGONZOLA, AND MOZZARELLA WITH BALSAMIC ONIONS PIZZA

You may be a little skeptical about putting pear on a pizza, but pear and blue cheese are a great combination—often used in salads. Here I use an Italian blue cheese, Gorgonzola, and balance the flavors with tangy balsamic onions and mild mozzarella.

2 pizza rounds of your choice

All-purpose flour for sprinkling

2 teaspoons extra-virgin olive oil

½ cup Balsamic Onions (see page 37)

4 ounces mozzarella cheese, shredded

2 ounces Gorgonzola cheese, crumbled

1 Roasted Pear (see page 48), thinly sliced

Kosher salt and freshly ground
  black pepper

1 One hour before baking, place a baking stone in the oven and preheat it to 500°F (450°F for gluten-free crusts).

2 Roll out 1 pizza round as thinly as possible and place it on a pizza peel sprinkled with flour. Leaving an outer lip all around the edge of the dough, cover the surface with half the oil; season with salt and pepper.

3 Evenly distribute half the onions on the dough. Top with half the cheeses and lay half the pear slices in a pinwheel pattern around the top.

4 Shake the peel lightly and slide the pizza onto the hot baking stone. Bake until browned, 6 to 7 minutes (10 to 14 minutes for gluten-free crusts).

5 Transfer the pizza to a firm surface and cut it into slices. Serve immediately.

6 Repeat all the steps using the second dough round.

SPINACH, ROASTED TOMATO SAUCE, AND MUSHROOM PIZZA

Sautéed spinach and seasoned mushrooms add complexity to this simple but satisfying pizza.

2 pizza rounds of your choice

All-purpose flour for sprinkling

2 teaspoons extra-virgin olive oil

½ teaspoon minced garlic

⅔ cup Roasted Tomato Sauce (see page 17)

6 ounces mozzarella cheese, shredded

½ cup Sautéed Spicy Spinach (see page 50)

1 cup Sautéed Mushrooms (see page 49)

2 tablespoons freshly grated Pecorino Romano or Parmesan cheese

Kosher salt and freshly ground black pepper

1 One hour before baking, place a baking stone in the oven and preheat it to 500°F (450°F for gluten-free crusts).

2 Roll out 1 pizza round as thinly as possible and place it on a pizza peel sprinkled with flour. Leaving an outer lip all around the edge of the dough, cover the surface with half the oil and garlic; season with salt and pepper.

3 Evenly spread half the sauce on the dough. Top with half each of the mozzarella, spinach, mushrooms, and Pecorino Romano.

4 Shake the peel lightly and slide the pizza onto the hot baking stone. Bake until browned, 6 to 7 minutes (10 to 14 minutes for gluten-free crusts).

5 Transfer the pizza to a firm surface and cut it into slices. Serve immediately.

6 Repeat all the steps using the second dough round.

CREAMY SPINACH AND PANEER NAAN PIZZA

Paneer is a fresh, mild cheese common in Southeast Asian cooking. This naan pizza is a nod to the traditional Indian dish of *saag paneer*, which contains spinach and paneer. My twist on this beloved Indian combo mixes together my creamy béchamel sauce with sautéed spinach for an incredibly satisfying treat! If you wish, you can also stir a teaspoon of garam masala into the sautéed spinach. If can't find paneer, substitute a queso blanco (look for one suitable for frying, often labeled *queso para freír*), or simply crumble a little feta on the pizza before it goes into the oven.

2 large rounds prepared naan bread (about 8 to 10 inches in diameter)

4 ounces prepared paneer cheese, cut into ½-inch cubes

All-purpose flour for sprinkling

1 cup Sautéed Spicy Spinach (page 50: add 1 teaspoon minced fresh ginger when you add the garlic)

1 cup Roasted Garlic Béchamel (see page 25)

4 ounces mozzarella cheese, shredded

¼ red onion, peeled and thinly sliced

Kosher salt and freshly ground black pepper

1 Preheat the oven to 450°F.

2 Place the rounds of naan on a half sheet pan.

3 In a small skillet, cook the paneer until lightly browned on all sides. Remove from the heat and set aside.

4 In a medium bowl, stir together the spinach and béchamel until well combined.

5 Evenly divide the spinach mixture between the naan rounds and top them with the mozzarella, paneer, and onion. Bake until browned, 8 to 10 minutes.

6 Transfer the pizzas to a firm surface and cut them into slices.

GARLICKY BROCCOLINI AND CHILE PIZZA

Broccoli's milder, more delicate relative, broccolini (aka baby broccoli), is perfect on a pizza. Since the spicy and garlicky broccolini topping already has chili in it, consider the fresh jalapeño for chili heads only. Shaved Parmesan nicely balances out the garlic and heat.

2 pizza rounds of your choice

All-purpose flour for sprinkling

2 teaspoons extra-virgin olive oil

½ teaspoon minced garlic

Kosher salt and freshly ground black pepper

1 cup Fresh Tomato Sauce (see page 20)

6 ounces mozzarella cheese, shredded

8 ounces Spicy and Garlicky Broccolini (see page 52), each piece halved

1 jalapeño pepper, sliced (optional)

½ ounce Parmesan cheese, shaved

1 One hour before baking, place a baking stone in the oven and preheat it to 500°F (450°F for gluten-free crusts).

2 Roll out 1 pizza round as thinly as possible and place it on a pizza peel sprinkled with flour. Leaving an outer lip all around the edge of the dough, cover the surface with half the oil and garlic; season with salt and pepper.

3 Evenly spread half the sauce on the dough. Top with half each of the mozzarella, broccolini, and jalapeño, if using.

4 Shake the peel lightly and slide the pizza onto the hot baking stone. Bake until browned, 6 to 7 minutes (10 to 14 minutes for gluten-free crusts). Scatter half the shaved Parmesan on top.

5 Transfer the pizza to a firm surface and cut it into slices. Serve immediately.

6 Repeat all the steps using the second dough round.

THREE-BROCCOLI PIZZA

If you can only find one or two kinds of broccoli, don't let that stop you from trying this pizza. With caramelized onions, béchamel, and two kinds of cheese, it has layers of amazing flavors. Chinese broccoli can usually be found in the produce section of Asian markets. Rapini (aka broccoli rabe) can be found at better supermarkets and gourmet markets.

2 pizza rounds of your choice

All-purpose flour for sprinkling

2/3 cup Béchamel Sauce (page 25, omitting the roasted garlic)

A few pieces each of rapini (broccoli rabe), Chinese broccoli, and broccoli florets

3/4 cup Caramelized Onions (see page 38)

4 ounces fresh mozzarella cheese, sliced

1/2 cup freshly grated Asiago cheese, plus a few shaved pieces for garnish

2 tablespoons extra-virgin olive oil

2 tablespoons garlic, thinly sliced and lightly toasted, for garnish

Kosher salt and freshly ground black pepper

1 One hour before baking, place a baking stone in the oven and preheat it to 500°F (450°F for gluten-free crusts).

2 Roll out 1 pizza round as thinly as possible and place it on a pizza peel sprinkled with flour. Leaving an outer lip all around the edge of the dough, season the surface with salt and pepper.

3 Evenly spread half the béchamel on the dough. Top with half each of the broccolis, onions, mozzarella, and Asiago. Drizzle with half the oil.

4 Shake the peel lightly and slide the pizza onto the hot baking stone. Bake until browned, 6 to 7 minutes (10 to 14 minutes for gluten-free crusts). Garnish with a few pieces of shaved Asiago and garlic chips.

5 Transfer the pizza to a firm surface and cut it into slices. Serve immediately.

6 Repeat all the steps using the second dough round.

BABA GHANOUSH FLATBREAD WITH GOAT CHEESE AND RED ONION

This Middle Eastern-inspired flatbread pairs smoky baba ghanoush with tart and creamy goat cheese. A few pomegranate seeds sprinkled on the finished pizza are a colorful and delicious touch.

2 pizza rounds of your choice

All-purpose flour for sprinkling

½ teaspoon minced garlic

1 cup Baba Ghanoush (see page 53)

4 ounces fresh goat cheese

¼ red onion, peeled and thinly sliced

Mint Oil (see page 28), for garnish

Pomegranate seeds, for garnish (optional)

Kosher salt and freshly ground black pepper

1 One hour before baking, place a baking stone in the oven and preheat it to 500°F (450°F for gluten-free crusts).

2 Roll out 1 pizza round as thinly as possible and place it on a pizza peel sprinkled with flour. Leaving an outer lip all around the edge of the dough, cover the surface with half the garlic; season with salt and pepper.

3 Top with half the baba ghanoush, dot with half the goat cheese, and top with half the onion.

4 Shake the peel lightly and slide the flatbread onto the hot baking stone. Bake until browned, 6 to 7 minutes (10 to 14 minutes for gluten-free crusts).

5 Transfer the flatbread to a firm surface and cut it into slices. Serve immediately, garnished with mint oil and pomegranate seeds, if desired.

6 Repeat all the steps using the second dough round.

RICOTTA AND CHERRY TOMATO PIZZA

The combination of ricotta and cherry tomatoes gives a marvelous freshness to this pizza, which is infused with two kinds of basil flavor—basil oil and fresh basil. When using the basil oil, be careful to keep a good lip on the crust to avoid the oil spilling over and scorching the baking stone.

2 pizza rounds of your choice

All-purpose flour for sprinkling

½ teaspoon minced garlic

1 tablespoon Basil Oil (see page 28)

4 ounces fresh mozzarella cheese, thinly sliced

⅓ cup ricotta cheese

1 pint cherry tomatoes, halved and seeded

2 tablespoons freshly grated Parmesan cheese

2 tablespoons chopped fresh basil, for garnish

Kosher salt and freshly ground black pepper

1 One hour before baking, place a baking stone in the oven and preheat it to 500°F (450°F for gluten-free crusts).

2 Roll out 1 pizza round as thinly as possible and place it on a pizza peel sprinkled with flour. Leaving an outer lip all around the edge of the dough, cover the surface with half the garlic; season with salt and pepper.

3 Evenly spread half the basil oil on the dough. Top with half the mozzarella and dot with half the ricotta. Evenly distribute half the tomatoes on top, then sprinkle with half the Parmesan.

4 Shake the peel lightly and slide the pizza onto the hot baking stone. Bake until browned, 6 to 7 minutes (10 to 14 minutes for gluten-free crusts).

5 Transfer the pizza to a firm surface and cut it into slices. Serve immediately, garnished with half the basil.

6 Repeat all the steps using the second dough round.

ROASTED CAULIFLOWER, MUSHROOM, AND RED ONION PIZZA

The secret to this pizza is the two kinds of garlic—roasted garlic in the creamy béchamel and fresh garlic on the pizza dough. Finish it with a drizzle of balsamic vinegar for a sweetly acidic balance to the delicate flavors of the other ingredients.

2 pizza rounds of your choice

All-purpose flour for sprinkling

½ teaspoon minced garlic

⅔ cup Cauliflower Purée (see page 54)

2 generous cups Roasted Cauliflower (see page 55)

¼ cup Sautéed Mushrooms (see page 49)

4 ounces mozzarella or Fontina cheese, shredded

¼ red onion, peeled and thinly sliced

2 tablespoons freshly grated Parmesan cheese

1 tablespoon chopped fresh flat-leaf parsley, for garnish

Balsamic vinegar, for garnish (optional)

Kosher salt and freshly ground black pepper

1 One hour before baking, place a baking stone in the oven and preheat it to 500°F (450°F for gluten-free crusts).

2 Roll out 1 pizza round as thinly as possible and place it on a pizza peel sprinkled with flour. Leaving an outer lip all around the edge of the dough, cover the surface with half the garlic; season with salt and pepper.

3 Evenly spread half the béchamel on the dough. Top with half each of the cauliflower, mushrooms, mozzarella, and onion. Sprinkle with half the Parmesan.

4 Shake the peel lightly and slide the pizza onto the hot baking stone. Bake until browned, 6 to 7 minutes (10 to 14 minutes for gluten-free crusts).

5 Transfer the pizza to a firm surface and garnish it with half the parsley and a drizzle of balsamic vinegar, if desired. Cut into slices and serve immediately.

6 Repeat all the steps using the second dough round.

CURRIED CAULIFLOWER NAAN PIZZA

Curried Cauliflower Naan Pizza packs in layers of flavors and textures, with sweet, curry-seasoned roasted cauliflower, roasted tomatoes, sliced jalapeño, and cooling yogurt.

- 2 large rounds prepared naan bread (about 8 to 10 inches in diameter)
- 2 cups Roasted Cauliflower (see page 55)
- 1 teaspoon curry powder, or 1 tablespoon curry paste from a jar (such as Patak's)
- 1 cup Roasted Tomatoes (see page 42), well drained

- 6 ounces mozzarella cheese, shredded
- 1 jalapeño pepper, seeded and sliced (optional)
- 1 tablespoon chopped fresh cilantro leaves, for garnish
- Plain yogurt or Herbed Yogurt Sauce (see page 32), for garnish (optional)

1 Preheat the oven to 450°F.

2 Place the rounds of naan on a half sheet pan.

3 In a medium bowl, toss the roasted cauliflower with the curry powder.

4 Evenly divide the tomatoes between the naan. Top with the mozzarella, cauliflower, and jalapeño, if using. Bake until browned, 8 to 10 minutes.

5 Transfer the pizzas to a firm surface and cut them into slices. Serve immediately, garnished with cilantro and yogurt, if desired.

RADICCHIO, ASIAGO, AND BALSAMIC ONION PIZZA

Radicchio, Asiago, and Balsamic Onion Pizza is great as it is, but you can also drape it with a few slices of thinly sliced prosciutto as soon as it comes out of the oven.

2 pizza rounds of your choice

All-purpose flour for sprinkling

2 teaspoons extra-virgin olive oil

½ teaspoon minced garlic

½ cup Balsamic Onions (see page 37)

2 ounces Asiago cheese, shredded

4 ounces mozzarella cheese, shredded

1½ cups thinly sliced radicchio

Kosher salt and freshly ground black pepper

1 One hour before baking, place a baking stone in the oven and preheat it to 500°F (450°F for gluten-free crusts).

2 Roll out 1 pizza round as thinly as possible and place it on a pizza peel sprinkled with flour. Leaving an outer lip all around the edge of the dough, cover the surface with half the oil and garlic; season with salt and pepper.

3 Evenly distribute half the onions on the dough. Top with half the cheeses and radicchio.

4 Shake the peel lightly and slide the pizza onto the hot baking stone. Bake until browned, 6 to 7 minutes (10 to 14 minutes for gluten-free crusts).

5 Transfer the pizza to a firm surface and cut it into slices. Serve immediately.

6 Repeat all the steps using the second dough round.

SUMMER SQUASH PIZZA

The freshness of summer on a pizza! If your farmers market carries different heirloom summer squashes, feel free to use them instead of the zucchini and yellow squash.

2 pizza rounds of your choice

All-purpose flour for sprinkling

2 teaspoons extra-virgin olive oil

½ teaspoon minced garlic

1 cup Fresh Tomato Sauce (see page 20), or ½ cup Traditional Basil Pesto (see page 23)

6 ounces fresh mozzarella cheese, shredded

1 small Grilled Zucchini (see page 47)

1 small Grilled Yellow Squash

⅓ cup sliced roasted red pepper from a jar (optional)

2 tablespoons freshly grated Parmesan cheese

Handful fresh basil leaves, torn, for garnish

Kosher salt and freshly ground black pepper

1 One hour before baking, place a baking stone in the oven and preheat it to 500°F (450°F for gluten-free crusts).

2 Roll out 1 pizza round as thinly as possible and place it on a pizza peel sprinkled with flour. Leaving an outer lip all around the edge of the dough, cover the surface with half the oil and garlic; season with salt and pepper.

3 Evenly spread half the tomato sauce on the dough. Top with half each of the mozzarella, zucchini, yellow squash, and red pepper, if using.

4 Shake the peel lightly and slide the pizza onto the hot baking stone. Bake until browned, 6 to 7 minutes (10 to 14 minutes for gluten-free crusts).

5 Transfer the pizza to a firm surface and cut it into slices. Serve immediately, garnished with half the basil.

6 Repeat all the steps using the second dough round.

EGGPLANT, OLIVE, CARAMELIZED ONIONS, AND TAHINI PIZZA

Eggplant, Olive, Caramelized Onions, and Tahini Pizza combines the deliciousness of Mediterranean and Middle Eastern flavors. The tahini sauce offers a creamy and tangy note on this cheese-optional pie.

2 pizza rounds of your choice

All-purpose flour for sprinkling

2 teaspoons extra-virgin olive oil

½ teaspoon minced garlic

½ cup Caramelized Onions (see page 38)

1 Roasted Eggplant (see page 45), thinly sliced

½ cup feta cheese, crumbled (optional)

¼ cup sliced oil-cured black olives (such as Kalamata)

¼ cup Tahini Sauce (see page 29), for garnish

2 teaspoons chopped fresh mint or parsley, for garnish

Kosher salt and freshly ground black pepper

1 One hour before baking, place a baking stone in the oven and preheat it to 500°F (450°F for gluten-free crusts).

2 Roll out 1 pizza round as thinly as possible and place it on a pizza peel sprinkled with flour. Leaving an outer lip all around the edge of the dough, cover the surface with half the oil and garlic; season with salt and pepper.

3 Evenly distribute half the onions and eggplant on top of the dough, then top with half the feta, if using, and half the olives.

4 Shake the peel lightly and slide the pizza onto the hot baking stone. Bake until browned, 6 to 7 minutes (10 to 14 minutes for gluten-free crusts).

5 Transfer the pizza to a firm surface and cut it into slices. Serve immediately, drizzled with half the tahini sauce and mint.

6 Repeat all the steps using the second dough round.

RED ONION, RICOTTA, AND SPINACH WITH FRESH TOMATO SAUCE PIZZA

Fresh mozzarella, spinach, and a simple tomato sauce—there's nothing fancy here, but it all works so well together.

2 pizza rounds of your choice

All-purpose flour for sprinkling

2 teaspoons extra-virgin olive oil

½ teaspoon minced garlic

1 cup Fresh Tomato Sauce (see page 20)

6 ounces fresh mozzarella cheese, pulled into small chunks

½ cup Sautéed Spicy Spinach (see page 50)

¼ cup diced red onion

½ cup ricotta cheese

Kosher salt and freshly ground black pepper

1 One hour before baking, place a baking stone in the oven and preheat it to 500°F (450°F for gluten-free crusts).

2 Roll out 1 pizza round as thinly as possible and place it on a pizza peel sprinkled with flour. Leaving an outer lip all around the edge of the dough, cover the surface with half the oil and garlic; season with salt and pepper.

3 Evenly spread half the tomato sauce on the dough. Top with half each of the mozzarella, spinach, and onion. Dot with half the ricotta.

4 Shake the peel lightly and slide the pizza onto the hot baking stone. Bake until browned, 6 to 7 minutes (10 to 14 minutes for gluten-free crusts).

5 Transfer the pizza to a firm surface and cut it into slices. Serve immediately.

6 Repeat all the steps using the second dough round.

ALMOND PESTO AND FRESH MOZZARELLA PIZZA

A very simple but delicious pizza—think of it as a Margherita pizza but with a pesto base.

2 pizza rounds of your choice

All-purpose flour for sprinkling

2 teaspoons extra-virgin olive oil

½ teaspoon minced garlic

½ cup Almond Pesto (see page 21) or Traditional Basil Pesto (see page 23)

6 ounces fresh mozzarella cheese, pulled into small chunks

2 plum tomatoes, thinly sliced and seeded

1 tablespoon freshly grated Parmesan cheese

Handful fresh basil leaves, for garnish

Kosher salt and freshly ground black pepper

1 One hour before baking, place a baking stone in the oven and preheat it to 500°F (450°F for gluten-free crusts).

2 Roll out 1 pizza round as thinly as possible and place it on a pizza peel sprinkled with flour. Leaving an outer lip all around the edge of the dough, cover the surface with half the oil and garlic; season with salt and pepper.

3 Evenly spread half the pesto on the dough. Top with half each of the mozzarella and tomato. Sprinkle with half the Parmesan.

4 Shake the peel lightly and slide the pizza onto the hot baking stone. Bake until browned, 6 to 7 minutes (10 to 14 minutes for gluten-free crusts).

5 Transfer the pizza to a firm surface and cut it into slices. Serve immediately, garnished with a few torn basil leaves.

6 Repeat all the steps using the second dough round.

CARAMELIZED ONION AND SWISS WITH THYME PIZZA

Inspired by the flavors of a savory French onion soup, Caramelized Onion and Swiss with Thyme Pizza is perfect with a green salad for lunch.

2 pizza rounds of your choice

All-purpose flour for sprinkling

2 teaspoons extra-virgin olive oil

½ teaspoon minced garlic

⅔ cup Caramelized Onions (see page 38)

5 ounces Gruyère, Jarlsberg, or Asiago cheese, shredded

1 tablespoon freshly grated Parmesan cheese

½ teaspoon chopped fresh thyme leaves

Balsamic vinegar, for garnish (optional)

Kosher salt and freshly ground black pepper

1 One hour before baking, place a baking stone in the oven and preheat it to 500°F (450°F for gluten-free crusts).

2 Roll out 1 pizza round as thinly as possible and place it on a pizza peel sprinkled with flour. Leaving an outer lip all around the edge of the dough, cover the surface with half the oil and garlic; season with salt and pepper.

3 Evenly distribute half the onions on the dough. Top with half each of the Gruyère, Parmesan, and thyme.

4 Shake the peel lightly and slide the pizza onto the hot baking stone. Bake until browned, 6 to 7 minutes (10 to 14 minutes for gluten-free crusts).

5 Transfer the pizza to a firm surface and cut it into slices. Serve immediately, drizzled with a little balsamic vinegar, if desired.

6 Repeat all the steps using the second dough round.

ROMESCO AND ZUCCHINI PIZZA

Romesco, a smoky Spanish roasted red pepper and nut sauce, is a natural with grilled vegetables. Here it's paired with chargrilled zucchini. For even more Spanish flair, replace some of the mozzarella with Manchego, an aged sheep's-milk cheese, and omit the Pecorino Romano.

2 pizza rounds of your choice

All-purpose flour for sprinkling

2 teaspoons extra-virgin olive oil

½ teaspoon minced garlic

½ cup Romesco Sauce (see page 24)

6 ounces mozzarella cheese, shredded

1 Grilled Zucchini (see page 47), thinly sliced

½ cup sliced roasted red peppers from a jar (optional)

1 tablespoon freshly grated Pecorino Romano cheese

2 teaspoons chopped fresh parsley, basil, or scallions, for garnish

Kosher salt and freshly ground black pepper

1 One hour before baking, place a baking stone in the oven and preheat it to 500°F (450°F for gluten-free crusts).

2 Roll out 1 pizza round as thinly as possible and place it on a pizza peel sprinkled with flour. Leaving an outer lip all around the edge of the dough, cover the surface with half the oil and garlic; season with salt and pepper.

3 Evenly spread half the sauce on the dough. Top with half each of the cheese, zucchini, and peppers, if using. Sprinkle with half the Pecorino.

4 Shake the peel lightly and slide the pizza onto the hot baking stone. Bake until browned, 6 to 7 minutes (10 to 14 minutes for gluten-free crusts).

5 Transfer the pizza to a firm surface and cut it into slices. Serve immediately, garnished with half the parsley.

6 Repeat all the steps using the second dough round.

BLACKENED BRUSSELS SPROUTS WITH PARMESAN PIZZA

Creamy garlic béchamel; nutty, smoky Brussels sprouts; and a little shaved Parmesan—this is definitely not your average pizza. Skip the anchovies to keep the pizza vegetarian.

2 pizza rounds of your choice

All-purpose flour for sprinkling

2 teaspoons extra-virgin olive oil

½ teaspoon minced garlic

⅔ cup Roasted Garlic Béchamel (see page 25)

½ pound Blackened Brussels Sprouts (see page 62)

1 to 2 ounces Parmesan cheese, shaved

4 to 5 anchovy fillets, rinsed if salt packed and broken into small bits (optional)

1 tablespoon chopped fresh parsley

Kosher salt and freshly ground black pepper

1 One hour before baking, place a baking stone in the oven and preheat it to 500°F (450°F for gluten-free crusts).

2 Roll out 1 pizza round as thinly as possible and place it on a pizza peel sprinkled with flour. Leaving an outer lip all around the edge of the dough, cover the surface with half the oil and garlic; season with salt and pepper.

3 Evenly spread half the béchamel on the dough. Top with half each of the Brussels sprouts and Parmesan. Top with half the anchovy bits, if using.

4 Shake the peel lightly and slide the pizza onto the hot baking stone. Bake until browned, 6 to 7 minutes (10 to 14 minutes for gluten-free crusts).

5 Transfer the pizza to a firm surface and cut it into slices. Serve immediately, garnished with half the parsley.

6 Repeat all the steps using the second dough round.

BROCCOLINI AND CHEDDAR PIZZA

There's something incredibly comforting about Broccolini and Cheddar Pizza. Maybe it's the echoes of that old-school broccoli and cheese side dish we all secretly love. Since this is rustic pizza, let's fancy things up a bit with tender broccolini (aka baby broccoli). Be sure to let the broccolini drain well after steaming it so it doesn't make the pizza soggy. (If your grocery store doesn't carry broccolini, or you don't want to be fancy, regular broccoli cut into bite-size florets will work just fine.) The mix of Cheddar and mozzarella helps ensure a good melt for the cheese.

2 teaspoons unsalted butter

¼ cup panko bread crumbs

2 pizza rounds of your choice

All-purpose flour for sprinkling

2 teaspoons extra-virgin olive oil

½ teaspoon minced garlic

1 (8-ounce) package broccolini (baby broccoli), trimmed, steamed, and cut into bite-size florets

6 ounces aged Cheddar cheese, shredded

2 ounces mozzarella cheese, shredded

Kosher salt and freshly ground black pepper

1 One hour before baking, place a baking stone in the oven and preheat it to 500°F (450°F for gluten-free crusts).

2 In a small skillet, melt the butter. Add the bread crumbs and toss to coat. Set aside.

3 Roll out 1 pizza round as thinly as possible and place it on a pizza peel sprinkled with flour. Leaving an outer lip all around the edge of the dough, cover the surface with half the oil and garlic; season with salt and pepper.

4 Evenly distribute half the broccolini and half the cheeses on the dough. Top with half the reserved bread crumbs.

5 Shake the peel lightly and slide the pizza onto the hot baking stone. Bake until browned, 6 to 7 minutes (10 to 14 minutes for gluten-free crusts).

6 Transfer the pizza to a firm surface and cut it into slices. Serve immediately.

7 Repeat all the steps (except step 2) using the second dough round.

TWO-SAUCE PIZZA

Pesto *and* tomato sauce? Absolutely. If you've got both on hand, you've got an extraordinarily satisfying—and quick—pizza just waiting for you. You can use any tomato sauce here, even your favorite variety from a jar (although it pains me to say it). A favorite!

2 pizza rounds of your choice

All-purpose flour for sprinkling

¼ cup Traditional Basil Pesto (see page 23) or Almond Pesto (see page 21)

8 ounces mozzarella cheese, shredded

⅔ cup tomato sauce, such as Marinara (see page 16), Fresh Tomato (see page 20), or Roasted Tomato (see page 17)

2 tablespoons coarsely grated or shaved Parmesan cheese

Kosher salt and freshly ground black pepper

1 One hour before baking, place a baking stone in the oven and preheat it to 500°F (450°F for gluten-free crusts).

2 Roll out 1 pizza round as thinly as possible and place it on a pizza peel sprinkled with flour. Leaving an outer lip all around the edge of the dough, season the surface with salt and pepper.

3 Evenly spread half the pesto on the dough. Top with half each of the mozzarella and the sauce. Sprinkle with half the Parmesan.

4 Shake the peel lightly and slide the pizza onto the hot baking stone. Bake until browned, 6 to 7 minutes (10 to 14 minutes for gluten-free crusts).

5 Transfer the pizza to a firm surface and cut it into slices. Serve immediately.

6 Repeat all the steps using the second dough round.

BURRATA, TOMATO, AND BASIL PIZZA

If you're not familiar with burrata, let me explain this heavenly delight. It's a fresh mozzarella cheese with a soft center filled with cheese curds and cream. It's very delicate, so don't break it open until the moment you're ready to use it. It also doesn't keep well, so use within a day of purchase. This is a supremely delicate pizza that doesn't need more than a few basil leaves for garnish, but if you twist my arm, I'd say that you could drape a thin slice or two of prosciutto on top as soon as it comes out of the oven.

2 pizza rounds of your choice

All-purpose flour for sprinkling

2 teaspoons extra-virgin olive oil

⅔ cup Fresh Tomato Sauce (see page 20)

1 (4- to 6-ounce) ball burrata

Handful fresh basil leaves, torn, for garnish

Kosher salt and freshly ground black pepper

1 One hour before baking, place a baking stone in the oven and preheat it to 500°F (450°F for gluten-free crusts).

2 Roll out 1 pizza round as thinly as possible and place it on a pizza peel sprinkled with flour. Leaving an outer lip along the edge of the dough, cover the surface with half the oil; season with salt and pepper.

3 Evenly spread half the sauce on the dough. Carefully break open the burrata ball and dot the surface evenly with half of it.

4 Shake the peel lightly and slide the pizza onto the hot baking stone. Bake until browned, 6 to 7 minutes (10 to 14 minutes for gluten-free crusts).

5 Transfer the pizza to a firm surface and cut it into slices. Serve immediately, garnished with half the basil.

6 Repeat all the steps using the second dough round.

5

MEAT PIZZAS

Meat pizzas are among many people's favorites. Some of these pizzas are iconic, like the pepperoni pizza. (Even the pizza emoji on the iPhone has pepperoni on it!) If you think a pizza isn't a pizza without pepperoni, check out the Bronx Bomber on page 126. This chapter pays homage to many of those traditional flavors, like Prosciutto and Arugula Pizza (see page 124), Meatball Pizza (see page 140), and Pepperoni, Red Onion, and Olive Pizza (see page 163), but it also combines ingredients in new, and perhaps unexpected, ways, such as with the Butternut Squash, Pancetta, Ricotta, and Red Onion Pizza (see page 174), Skirt Steak and Chimichurri Pizza (see page 147), and Roasted Pulled Chicken, Provolone, and Basil Oil Pizza (see page 142).

PROSCIUTTO AND ARUGULA PIZZA

A classic rustic pizza. Why mess with what works? Definitely spring for the fresh mozzarella, or even buffalo mozzarella, because the quality of each ingredient is essential. The arugula and prosciutto are added when the pizza comes out of the oven; the heat wilts the arugula and starts to melt the fat on the prosciutto.

2 pizza rounds of your choice

All-purpose flour for sprinkling

2 teaspoons extra-virgin olive oil

½ teaspoon minced garlic

⅔ cup Fresh Tomato Sauce (see page 20)

8 ounces fresh mozzarella, pulled into small pieces

2 tablespoons freshly grated Parmesan cheese

4 ounces prosciutto, very thinly sliced

2 cups baby arugula (about 2½ ounces)

Kosher salt and freshly ground black pepper

1 One hour before baking, place a baking stone in the oven and preheat it to 500°F (450°F for gluten-free crusts).

2 Roll out 1 pizza round as thinly as possible and place it on a pizza peel sprinkled with flour. Leaving an outer lip all around the edge of the dough, cover the surface with half the oil and garlic; season with salt and pepper.

3 Evenly spread half the sauce on the dough. Dot with half the mozzarella. Sprinkle with half the Parmesan.

4 Shake the peel lightly and slide the pizza onto the hot baking stone. Bake until browned, 6 to 7 minutes (10 to 14 minutes for gluten-free crusts). As soon as the pizza comes out of the oven, drape it with half the prosciutto slices.

5 Transfer the pizza to a firm surface and cut it into slices. Serve immediately, topped with half the arugula.

6 Repeat all the steps using the second dough round.

BRONX BOMBER

A pizza for the pepperoni purists among us. If you love a pizza with a lot of cheese and pepperoni, you'll likely agree that the Bronx Bomber hits it out of the park.

2 pizza rounds of your choice

All-purpose flour for sprinkling

2 teaspoons extra-virgin olive oil

½ teaspoon minced garlic

1 cup Marinara Sauce (see page 16)

10 ounces mozzarella cheese, shredded

5 ounces pepperoni, thinly sliced

Handful fresh basil leaves, torn, for garnish

Kosher salt and freshly ground
    black pepper

1 One hour before baking, place a baking stone in the oven and preheat it to 500°F (450°F for gluten-free crusts).

2 Roll out 1 pizza round as thinly as possible and place it on a pizza peel sprinkled with flour. Leaving an outer lip all around the edge of the dough, cover the surface with half the oil and garlic; season with salt and pepper.

3 Evenly spread half the sauce on the dough. Top with half each of the mozzarella and the pepperoni.

4 Shake the peel lightly and slide the pizza onto the hot baking stone. Bake until browned, 6 to 7 minutes (10 to 14 minutes for gluten-free crusts).

5 Transfer the pizza to a firm surface and cut it into slices. Serve immediately, topped with half the basil.

6 Repeat all the steps using the second dough round.

FIG AND PROSCIUTTO PIZZA

Topped with a sweet and savory homemade fig jam, Gorgonzola, and prosciutto, Fig and Prosciutto Pizza is a surprising symphony of flavors that all work magic together.

2 pizza rounds of your choice

All-purpose flour for sprinkling

2 teaspoons extra-virgin olive oil

½ teaspoon minced garlic

1 teaspoon chopped fresh rosemary leaves

½ cup Fig Jam (see page 57)

4 ounces Gorgonzola cheese, crumbled

3 ounces prosciutto, very thinly sliced

1 scallion, thinly sliced lengthwise, for garnish

Kosher salt and freshly ground black pepper

1 One hour before baking, place a baking stone in the oven and preheat it to 500°F (450°F for gluten-free crusts).

2 Roll out 1 pizza round as thinly as possible and place it on a pizza peel sprinkled with flour. Leaving an outer lip all around the edge of the dough, cover the surface with half each of the oil, garlic, and rosemary; season with salt and pepper.

3 Evenly dot half the fig jam and Gorgonzola on the dough. Top with half the prosciutto slices.

4 Shake the peel lightly and slide the pizza onto the hot baking stone. Bake until browned, 6 to 7 minutes (10 to 14 minutes for gluten-free crusts).

5 Transfer the pizza to a firm surface and cut it into slices. Serve immediately, garnished with half the scallion slices.

6 Repeat all the steps using the second dough round.

KIELBASA, SAUERKRAUT, POTATO, AND MUSTARD AIOLI PIZZA

You're putting *what* on a pizza? I know, I know, but you'll just have to trust me on this one. Somehow kielbasa, sauerkraut, and potato just work together. Don't be surprised if you and your family end up agreeing with me.

2 pizza rounds of your choice

All-purpose flour for sprinkling

2 teaspoons extra-virgin olive oil

½ teaspoon minced garlic

6 ounces kielbasa, thinly sliced

½ cup sauerkraut

4 boiled or roasted new potatoes, thinly sliced

2 ounces aged Provolone cheese, shredded

4 teaspoons freshly grated Parmesan cheese

1 scallion, thinly sliced lengthwise, for garnish

Mustard Aioli (see page 34), for garnish

Kosher salt and freshly ground black pepper

1 One hour before baking, place a baking stone in the oven and preheat it to 500°F (450°F for gluten-free crusts).

2 Roll out 1 pizza round as thinly as possible and place it on a pizza peel sprinkled with flour. Leaving an outer lip all around the edge of the dough, cover the surface with half the oil and garlic; season with salt and pepper.

3 Evenly distribute half the kielbasa on the dough. Top with half each of the sauerkraut, potatoes, and Provolone. Sprinkle with half the Parmesan.

4 Shake the peel lightly and slide the pizza onto the hot baking stone. Bake until browned, 6 to 7 minutes (10 to 14 minutes for gluten-free crusts).

5 Transfer the pizza to a firm surface and cut it into slices. Serve immediately, garnished with half the scallion slices and lightly drizzled with Mustard Aioli.

6 Repeat all the steps using the second dough round.

KIELBASA, RED ONION, AND CABBAGE PIZZA

There's nothing fancy about Kielbasa, Red Onion, and Cabbage Pizza; it's just delicious. The cabbage adds a sweetness and crunch, the kielbasa a lovely smokiness, and the blend of cheeses comforting satisfaction.

2 pizza rounds of your choice

All-purpose flour for sprinkling

2 teaspoons extra-virgin olive oil

½ teaspoon minced garlic

3 ounces aged Cheddar cheese

3 ounces Monterey Jack or other mild

melting cheese

6 ounces kielbasa, sliced into 16 rounds

½ red onion, peeled and thinly sliced

1 cup very thinly sliced red cabbage

Kosher salt and freshly ground black pepper

1 One hour before baking, place a baking stone in the oven and preheat it to 500°F (450°F for gluten-free crusts).

2 Roll out 1 pizza round as thinly as possible and place it on a pizza peel sprinkled with flour. Leaving an outer lip all around the edge of the dough, cover the surface with half the oil and garlic; season with salt and pepper.

3 Evenly distribute half the cheeses on the dough. Top with half each of the kielbasa, onion, and cabbage.

4 Shake the peel lightly and slide the pizza onto the hot baking stone. Bake until browned, 6 to 7 minutes (10 to 14 minutes for gluten-free crusts).

5 Transfer the pizza to a firm surface and cut it into slices. Serve immediately.

6 Repeat all the steps using the second dough round.

JAMÓN SERRANO AND ROMESCO WITH SHAVED MANCHEGO PIZZA

Viva España! Spanish cured ham, a traditional Spanish red pepper sauce, and Spanish sheep's milk cheese make this pizza an ode to the Iberian peninsula.

2 pizza rounds of your choice

All-purpose flour for sprinkling

½ teaspoon minced garlic

½ cup Romesco Sauce (see page 24)

4 ounces mozzarella cheese, shredded

2 ounces Manchego cheese, grated

3 ounces Jamón Serrano or prosciutto, thinly sliced

Kosher salt and freshly ground black pepper

---

1 One hour before baking, place a baking stone in the oven and preheat it to 500°F (450°F for gluten-free crusts).

2 Roll out 1 pizza round as thinly as possible and place it on a pizza peel sprinkled with flour. Leaving an outer lip all around the edge of the dough, cover the surface with half the garlic; season with salt and pepper.

3 Evenly spread half the sauce on the dough. Top with half each of the mozzarella, Manchego, and Jamón Serrano.

4 Shake the peel lightly and slide the pizza onto the hot baking stone. Bake until browned, 6 to 7 minutes (10 to 14 minutes for gluten-free crusts).

5 Transfer the pizza to a firm surface and cut it into slices. Serve immediately.

6 Repeat all the steps using the second dough round.

ISABELLE'S PIZZA

Topped with lots of crave-worthy ingredients like caramelized onions, Virginia ham, fresh asparagus, and Provolone, Isabelle's Pizza is a masterpiece of flavor and texture.

2 pizza rounds of your choice

All-purpose flour for sprinkling

2 teaspoons extra-virgin olive oil

½ teaspoon minced garlic

¼ pound Virginia ham, thinly sliced

8 thin asparagus spears, blanched and sliced lengthwise

½ cup Caramelized Onions (see page 38)

8 ounces Provolone cheese, shredded

2 tablespoons freshly grated Parmesan cheese

1 scallion, thinly sliced lengthwise, for garnish

Kosher salt and freshly ground black pepper

1 One hour before baking, place a baking stone in the oven and preheat it to 500°F (450°F for gluten-free crusts).

2 Roll out 1 pizza round as thinly as possible and place it on a pizza peel sprinkled with flour. Leaving an outer lip all around the edge of the dough, cover the surface with half the oil and garlic; season with salt and pepper.

3 Evenly distribute half the ham on the dough (it is not necessary to cover the surface completely). Top with the half each of the asparagus and caramelized onions, then cover with half the Provolone. Sprinkle with half the Parmesan.

4 Shake the peel lightly and slide the pizza onto the hot baking stone. Bake until browned, 6 to 7 minutes (10 to 14 minutes for gluten-free crusts).

5 Transfer the pizza to a firm surface and cut it into slices. Serve immediately, garnished with half the scallions.

6 Repeat all the steps using the second dough round.

ROASTED CAULIFLOWER AND BACON PIZZA

Cauliflower, like Brussels sprouts and other veggies, is a perfect complement to bacon. Here I double up on the cauliflower by using a rich cauliflower purée in place of the sauce and top with blanched cauliflower florets. Who said pizza can't be both healthy(*ish*) and delicious?

2 pizza rounds of your choice

All-purpose flour for sprinkling

1 cup Cauliflower Purée (see page 54)

3 cups cauliflower florets (from 1 large head cauliflower), blanched until tender

½ cup Caramelized Onions (see page 38)

6 ounces fresh mozzarella cheese, thinly sliced

½ cup (about 1 ½ ounces) packed baby spinach leaves

2 slices thick-cut bacon (preferably applewood smoked), sliced into ¼-inch- wide strips ("lardons") and cooked

2 tablespoons freshly grated Parmesan cheese

2 tablespoons Tomato Oil (see page 27) or extra-virgin olive oil, for drizzling

Kosher salt and freshly ground black pepper

1 One hour before baking, place a baking stone in the oven and preheat it to 500°F (450°F for gluten-free crusts).

2 Roll out 1 pizza round as thinly as possible and place it on a pizza peel sprinkled with flour. Leaving an outer lip all around the edge of the dough, season the surface with salt and pepper.

3 Evenly spread half the cauliflower purée on the dough. Top with half each of the florets, onions, mozzarella, spinach, lardons, and Parmesan.

4 Shake the peel lightly and slide the pizza onto the hot baking stone. Bake until browned, 6 to 7 minutes (10 to 14 minutes for gluten-free crusts).

5 Transfer the pizza to a firm surface, drizzle it with half the tomato oil, and cut it into slices. Serve immediately.

6 Repeat all the steps using the second dough round.

CHICKEN CHILI PIZZA

This Southwest-inspired pizza uses a deliciously spicy chicken chili that is tempered by mild cheeses and sour cream. Feel free to top it with hot sauce or sliced jalapeños if you want more heat.

2 pizza rounds of your choice

All-purpose flour for sprinkling

3 ounces Cheddar cheese, shredded

3 ounces Monterey Jack cheese, shredded

1 cup Chicken Chili (see page 60)

¼ cup Caramelized Onions (see page 38)

Sour cream, for garnish

2 tablespoons chopped scallions, for garnish

Kosher salt and freshly ground black pepper

1 One hour before baking, place a baking stone in the oven and preheat it to 500°F (450°F for gluten-free crusts).

2 Roll out 1 pizza round as thinly as possible and place it on a pizza peel sprinkled with flour. Leaving an outer lip all around the edge of the dough, season the surface with salt and pepper.

3 Evenly distribute half each of the cheeses, chili, and onions on the dough.

4 Shake the peel lightly and slide the pizza onto the hot baking stone. Bake until browned, 6 to 7 minutes (10 to 14 minutes for gluten-free crusts).

5 Transfer the pizza to a firm surface, garnish it with dollops of sour cream and half the scallions, and cut it into slices. Serve immediately.

6 Repeat all the steps using the second dough round.

OLD-FASHIONED MEAT LOVER'S BOLOGNESE PIZZA

Slow-cooked Bolognese sauce topped with ricotta, mozzarella, pepperoni, prosciutto, and sausage—what's not to love?

2 pizza rounds of your choice

All-purpose flour for sprinkling

1 cup Bolognese Sauce (see page 18)

¼ cup ricotta cheese

4 ounces fresh mozzarella cheese, thinly sliced

1 ounce pepperoni (about 14 slices)

1 ounce prosciutto (2 to 3 thin slices), roughly torn

1 link Italian sausage, cooked and crumbled

A few fresh basil leaves, torn, for garnish

Extra-virgin olive oil, for garnish

Kosher salt and freshly ground black pepper

1 One hour before baking, place a baking stone in the oven and preheat it to 500°F (450°F for gluten-free crusts).

2 Roll out 1 pizza round as thinly as possible and place it on a pizza peel sprinkled with flour. Leaving an outer lip all around the edge of the dough, season the surface with salt and pepper.

3 Evenly spread half the sauce on the dough. Top with half each of the ricotta and mozzarella, then half each of the pepperoni, prosciutto, and sausage. Add a few pieces of torn basil and a drizzle of oil.

4 Shake the peel lightly and slide the pizza onto the hot baking stone. Bake until browned, 6 to 7 minutes (10 to 14 minutes for gluten-free crusts).

5 Transfer the pizza to a firm surface and cut it into slices. Serve immediately.

6 Repeat all the steps using the second dough round.

SPICY CHICKEN SAUSAGE PIZZA

Chicken sausage is often a little leaner than its beef or pork counterparts, but what is lost in fat is made up for in the flavor of the spicy sausage, tangy balsamic onions, and just a hint of decadence from the ricotta.

2 pizza rounds of your choice

All-purpose flour for sprinkling

2 teaspoons extra-virgin olive oil

½ teaspoon minced garlic

⅔ cup Marinara Sauce (see page 16)

6 ounces (about 1½ links) spicy chicken sausage, cooked and crumbled

½ cup Balsamic Onions (see page 37)

½ cup Herbed Ricotta Cheese (see page 41)

Kosher salt and freshly ground black pepper

1 One hour before baking, place a baking stone in the oven and preheat it to 500°F (450°F for gluten-free crusts).

2 Roll out 1 pizza round as thinly as possible and place it on a pizza peel sprinkled with flour. Leaving an outer lip all around the edge of the dough, cover the surface with half the oil and garlic; season with salt and pepper.

3 Evenly spread half the sauce on the dough. Top with half each of the sausage and onions. Dot with half the ricotta.

4 Shake the peel lightly and slide the pizza onto the hot baking stone. Bake until browned, 6 to 7 minutes (10 to 14 minutes for gluten-free crusts).

5 Transfer the pizza to a firm surface and cut it into slices. Serve immediately.

6 Repeat all the steps using the second dough round.

TUSCAN FLATBREAD

Tuscan Flatbread is a variation on the Fig and Prosciutto Pizza (see page 127), but with more olive oil and Fontina cheese. It's also baked at a slightly lower oven temperature. To keep the toppings from scorching your baking stone, you might want to prep the flatbread on a piece of high-temperature parchment paper that you can slide onto the stone.

2 pizza rounds of your choice

All-purpose flour for sprinkling

¼ cup extra-virgin olive oil

7 to 8 slices Fontina cheese

½ cup Fig Jam (see page 57)

4 ounces Gorgonzola cheese, crumbled

1 teaspoon chopped fresh rosemary

7 to 8 slices prosciutto (about 4 ounces)

1 One hour before baking, place a baking stone in the oven and preheat it to 450°F.

2 Roll out 1 pizza round as thinly as possible and place it on a pizza peel sprinkled with flour.

3 Evenly drizzle half the oil over the flatbread. Top with half the Fontina, then spread half the jam over the Fontina. Top with half each of the Gorgonzola and rosemary.

4 Shake the peel lightly and slide the flatbread onto the hot baking stone. Bake until browned, 8 to 10 minutes.

5 Transfer the flatbread to a firm surface, drape it with half the prosciutto slices, and cut it into slices. Serve immediately.

6 Repeat all the steps using the second dough round.

MEATBALL PIZZA

Are there two greater words in the English language than *meatball* and *pizza*? Yes, when you combine them to make Meatball Pizza. This is a pizza you want to keep simple—just crust, sauce, cheese, and tender, moist meatballs packed with flavor. I give some different sauce options below, but I wouldn't change much else.

2 pizza rounds of your choice

All-purpose flour for sprinkling

2 teaspoons extra-virgin olive oil

½ teaspoon minced garlic

⅔ cup Marinara Sauce (see page 16) or Fresh Tomato Sauce (see page 20) or Roasted Tomato Sauce (see page 17)

8 ounces mozzarella cheese, shredded

6 to 8 Italian Meatballs (see page 61), sliced in half

½ cup freshly grated Parmesan cheese

Kosher salt and freshly ground black pepper

1 One hour before baking, place a baking stone in the oven and preheat it to 500°F (450°F for gluten-free crusts).

2 Roll out 1 pizza round as thinly as possible and place it on a pizza peel sprinkled with flour. Leaving an outer lip all around the edge of the dough, cover the surface with half the oil and garlic; season with salt and pepper.

3 Evenly spread half the sauce on the dough. Top with half each of the mozzarella, meatballs, and Parmesan.

4 Shake the peel lightly and slide the pizza onto the hot baking stone. Bake until browned, 6 to 7 minutes (10 to 14 minutes for gluten-free crusts).

5 Transfer the pizza to a firm surface and cut it into slices. Serve immediately.

6 Repeat all the steps using the second dough round.

SALSA VERDE CHICKEN AND QUESO QUESADILLA PIZZA

You may think of quesadillas simply as cheesy filled tortillas, but *queso quesadilla* is a delicious type of creamy Mexican melting cheese. It's very mild and perfect on this pizza with a tangy tomatillo-based salsa verde. A crowd pleaser!

2 pizza rounds of your choice

All-purpose flour for sprinkling

2 teaspoons extra-virgin olive oil

½ teaspoon minced garlic

⅔ cup Mexican salsa verde from a jar

½ pound cooked boneless, skinless chicken (any combination of light and dark meat), shredded into bite-size pieces

6 ounces *queso quesadilla* or Monterey Jack cheese

1 plum tomato, seeded, cored, and diced

¼ cup chopped red onion

2 tablespoons chopped fresh cilantro or scallions, for garnish

Sour cream, for garnish (optional)

Sliced serrano chilis or pickled jalapeño slices, for garnish (optional)

Kosher salt and freshly ground black pepper

1 One hour before baking, place a baking stone in the oven and preheat it to 500°F (450°F for gluten-free crusts).

2 Roll out 1 pizza round as thinly as possible and place it on a pizza peel sprinkled with flour. Leaving an outer lip all around the edge of the dough, cover the surface with half the oil and garlic; season with salt and pepper.

3 Evenly spread half the salsa verde on the dough. Top with half each of the chicken, cheese, tomato, and onion.

4 Shake the peel lightly and slide the pizza onto the hot baking stone. Bake until browned, 6 to 7 minutes (10 to 14 minutes for gluten-free crusts).

5 Transfer the pizza to a firm surface and cut it into slices. Serve immediately, garnished with half the cilantro, and a dollop of sour cream and half the chilis, if desired.

6 Repeat all the steps using the second dough round.

ROASTED PULLED CHICKEN, PROVOLONE, AND BASIL OIL PIZZA

Roast chicken is a meal that keeps on giving, and one of its main gifts is leftovers. There are hundreds of uses for leftover chicken, and you may not have considered that pizza is one of them. The ingredient list calls for a half pound of cooked chicken, but you can add more or less depending on what you've got on hand. You could experiment with different cheeses as well. Be sure to keep a good lip on the crust so that the basil oil doesn't spill off and burn on the baking stone.

2 pizza rounds of your choice

All-purpose flour for sprinkling

½ teaspoon minced garlic

2 tablespoons Basil Oil (see page 28), plus additional for garnish

6 ounces Provolone cheese, shredded

½ pound cooked boneless, skinless chicken (any combination of light and dark meat), pulled into bite-size pieces

Kosher salt and freshly ground black pepper

1 One hour before baking, place a baking stone in the oven and preheat it to 500°F (450°F for gluten-free crusts).

2 Roll out 1 pizza round as thinly as possible and place it on a pizza peel sprinkled with flour. Leaving an outer lip all around the edge of the dough, cover the surface with half the garlic; season with salt and pepper.

3 Evenly spread half the basil oil on the dough. Top with half each of the Provolone and chicken pieces.

4 Shake the peel lightly and slide the pizza onto the hot baking stone. Bake until browned, 6 to 7 minutes (10 to 14 minutes for gluten-free crusts).

5 Transfer the pizza to a firm surface and cut it into slices. Serve immediately, drizzled with half the basil oil.

6 Repeat all the steps using the second dough round.

CHICKEN, ALMOND PESTO, AND ARUGULA PIZZA

A deliciously simple pizza easy enough for a busy weeknight. Chicken and pesto taste great together, and with the arugula on top, it's a complete meal.

½ pound cooked boneless, skinless chicken (any combination of light and dark meat), shredded into bite-size pieces

⅓ cup Almond Pesto (see page 21) or Basil Pesto (see page 23)

2 pizza rounds of your choice

All-purpose flour for sprinkling

6 ounces mozzarella cheese, shredded

3 tablespoons freshly grated Parmesan or Pecorino Romano cheese

2 cups baby arugula (about 2½ ounces)

Kosher salt and freshly ground black pepper

1 One hour before baking, place a baking stone in the oven and preheat it to 500°F (450°F for gluten-free crusts).

2 Toss the chicken pieces with 2 tablespoons of the pesto. Set aside.

3 Roll out 1 pizza round as thinly as possible and place it on a pizza peel sprinkled with flour. Leaving an outer lip all around the edge of the dough, season the surface with salt and pepper.

4 Evenly spread half the remaining pesto on the dough. Top with half each of the chicken, mozzarella, and Parmesan.

5 Shake the peel lightly and slide the pizza onto the hot baking stone. Bake until browned, 6 to 7 minutes (10 to 14 minutes for gluten-free crusts).

6 Transfer the pizza to a firm surface and top it with half the arugula, then cut it into slices. Serve immediately.

7 Repeat all the steps (except step 2) using the second dough round.

SWEET ITALIAN SAUSAGE AND FENNEL PIZZA

Italian sausage contains fennel seed, so it's no surprise that it works well with fresh fennel! If you don't have time to braise the fennel, you can thinly slice half a raw bulb and place the slices right on the pizza. Either way, it will be delicious.

2 pizza rounds of your choice

All-purpose flour for sprinkling

2 teaspoons extra-virgin olive oil

½ teaspoon minced garlic

⅔ cup Marinara Sauce (see page 16)

6 ounces Fontina cheese, shredded

6 ounces (about 1½ links) sweet Italian sausage, cooked and crumbled

¾ cup Braised Fennel (see page 40), well drained

8 cloves Roasted Garlic (see page 36), roughly chopped

Kosher salt and freshly ground black pepper

1 One hour before baking, place a baking stone in the oven and preheat it to 500°F (450°F for gluten-free crusts).

2 Roll out 1 pizza round as thinly as possible and place it on a pizza peel sprinkled with flour. Leaving an outer lip all around the edge of the dough, cover the surface with half the oil and garlic; season with salt and pepper.

3 Evenly spread half the sauce on the dough. Top with half each of the Fontina, sausage, fennel, and garlic.

4 Shake the peel lightly and slide the pizza onto the hot baking stone. Bake until browned, 6 to 7 minutes (10 to 14 minutes for gluten-free crusts).

5 Transfer the pizza to a firm surface and cut it into slices. Serve immediately.

6 Repeat all the steps using the second dough round.

CHORIZO, RED PEPPER, AND MANCHEGO PIZZA

This Spanish-inspired pizza has the can't-go-wrong flavor combination of chorizo, red pepper, and Manchego.

2 pizza rounds of your choice

All-purpose flour for sprinkling

2 teaspoons extra-virgin olive oil

½ teaspoon minced garlic

⅔ cup Roasted Tomato Sauce (see page 17)

4 ounces mozzarella cheese, shredded

2 ounces Manchego cheese, shaved

5 ounces dried Spanish chorizo, very thinly sliced

½ red bell pepper, seeded and diced, or ⅓ cup diced roasted red pepper from a jar

2 teaspoons chopped fresh parsley or scallions, for garnish

Kosher salt and freshly ground black pepper

1 One hour before baking, place a baking stone in the oven and preheat it to 500°F (450°F for gluten-free crusts).

2 Roll out 1 pizza round as thinly as possible and place it on a pizza peel sprinkled with flour. Leaving an outer lip all around the edge of the dough, cover the surface with half the oil and garlic; season with salt and pepper.

3 Evenly spread half the sauce on the dough. Top with half each of the cheeses, chorizo, and bell pepper.

4 Shake the peel lightly and slide the pizza onto the hot baking stone. Bake until browned, 6 to 7 minutes (10 to 14 minutes for gluten-free crusts).

5 Transfer the pizza to a firm surface and cut it into slices. Serve immediately, garnished with half the parsley.

6 Repeat all the steps using the second dough round.

SKIRT STEAK AND CHIMICHURRI PIZZA

Seared, thinly sliced marinated steak, herby Chimichurri Sauce, and fresh mozzarella (to sop up all the flavors) make a standout Argentinian-inspired pizza.

½ pound skirt steak

¼ cup plus 2 tablespoons Chimichurri Sauce (see page 26)

2 pizza rounds of your choice

All-purpose flour for sprinkling

½ teaspoon minced garlic

Kosher salt and freshly ground black pepper

8 ounces buffalo or fresh mozzarella cheese, thinly sliced

2 teaspoons freshly grated Parmesan cheese

1 tablespoon chopped fresh parsley, for garnish

1 In a zip-top plastic bag, place the steak and ¼ cup of the Chimichurri Sauce. Refrigerate for at least 1 hour and up to overnight to marinate.

2 One hour before baking, place a baking stone in the oven and preheat it to 500°F (450°F for gluten-free crusts).

3 Remove the steak from the marinade, shaking off the excess. Heat a skillet over high heat, and cook the steak, uncovered, until well-browned, 2 to 3 minutes per side. Let rest 5 minutes before slicing it against the grain into ¼-inch-thick slices.

4 Roll out 1 pizza round as thinly as possible and place it on a pizza peel sprinkled with flour. Leaving an outer lip all around the edge of the dough, cover the surface with half the garlic; season with salt and pepper.

5 Evenly place half the mozzarella on the dough. Top with half of the Parmesan.

6 Shake the peel lightly and slide the pizza onto the hot baking stone. Bake until browned, 6 to 7 minutes (10 to 14 minutes for gluten-free crusts).

7 Transfer the pizza to a firm surface, add half of the steak, and drizzle with 1 tablespoon of the Chimichurri, and cut it into slices. Sprinkle with parsley and serve immediately.

8 Repeat all the steps (except steps 1 and 3) using the second dough round.

DECONSTRUCTED CARBONARA FLATBREAD

Spaghetti carbonara is a classic Italian dish made of pancetta (or bacon), cream, Parmesan, and eggs. It's so beloved that it's not uncommon to hear people say it would be their choice for a last meal. (*New Yorker* writer Calvin Trillin once famously argued that spaghetti carbonara should replace turkey on Thanksgiving.) "Deconstructed carbonara" sounds fancy, but it just means that I've taken most of the main carbonara ingredients and used them to top this fantastic pizza. Be sure to cook the egg so that there's still a little jiggle in the yolk so you can break it and mop it up with the crust.

4 ounces pancetta, diced, or thick-cut bacon, sliced into ¼-inch-long narrow strips ("lardons")

2 pizza rounds of your choice

All-purpose flour for sprinkling

2 teaspoons extra-virgin olive oil

½ teaspoon minced garlic

½ cup Caramelized Onions (see page 38)

¼ cup freshly grated Pecorino Romano cheese, plus a few shavings for garnish

4 large eggs, fried or sunny side up

Kosher salt and coarsely cracked black pepper

1 One hour before baking, place a baking stone in the oven and preheat it to 500°F (450°F for gluten-free crusts).

2 In a large skillet over medium-low heat, cook the pancetta until browned, 8 to 10 minutes. Transfer to a paper towel-lined plate to drain.

3 Roll out 1 pizza round as thinly as possible and place it on a pizza peel sprinkled with flour. Leaving an outer lip all around the edge of the dough, cover the surface with half the oil and garlic; season with salt and pepper.

4 Evenly distribute half each of the onions, Pecorino Romano, and pancetta on the dough.

5 Shake the peel lightly and slide the pizza onto the hot baking stone. Bake until browned, 6 to 7 minutes (10 to 14 minutes for gluten-free crusts). Top with eggs.

6 Repeat all the steps (except steps 2 and 6) using the second dough round.

MERGUEZ FLATBREAD WITH HERBED YOGURT SAUCE AND MINT OIL

Merguez is a spicy North African lamb sausage. The herbed yogurt sauce and mint oil provide a cooling balance to the other strong flavors.

2 pizza rounds of your choice

All-purpose flour for sprinkling

½ teaspoon minced garlic

2 ounces Manchego cheese, shaved

½ pound merguez sausage, cooked and thinly sliced

½ cup sliced roasted red bell peppers from a jar

⅓ cup Herbed Yogurt Sauce (see page 32), or more to taste

2 tablespoons Mint Oil (see page 28), or 2 teaspoons chopped fresh mint

Kosher salt and freshly ground black pepper

1 One hour before baking, place a baking stone in the oven and preheat it to 500°F (450°F for gluten-free crusts).

2 Roll out 1 pizza round as thinly as possible and place it on a pizza peel sprinkled with flour. Leaving an outer lip all around the edge of the dough, cover the surface with half the garlic; season with salt and pepper.

3 Evenly distribute half each of the Manchego, sausage, and peppers on the dough.

4 Shake the peel lightly and slide the pizza onto the hot baking stone. Bake until browned, 6 to 7 minutes (10 to 14 minutes for gluten-free crusts).

5 Transfer the pizza to a firm surface, garnish it with half the yogurt sauce and mint oil, and cut it into slices. Serve immediately.

6 Repeat all the steps using the second dough round.

HAM AND CHEESE FLATBREAD

Do you like your ham and cheese with tomato? If so, I've got you covered. There's nothing fancy here, but you're going to love it.

2 pizza rounds of your choice

All-purpose flour for sprinkling

2 teaspoons extra-virgin olive oil

½ teaspoon minced garlic

3 ounces aged Cheddar cheese, shredded

3 ounces mozzarella cheese, shredded

¼ pound Virginia ham or deli ham, thinly sliced

2 plum tomatoes, sliced and seeded (optional)

Mustard Aioli (see page 34) or Dijon mustard, for garnish

Kosher salt and freshly ground black pepper

1 One hour before baking, place a baking stone in the oven and preheat it to 500°F (450°F for gluten-free crusts).

2 Roll out 1 pizza round as thinly as possible and place it on a pizza peel sprinkled with flour. Leaving an outer lip all around the edge of the dough, cover the surface with half the oil and garlic; season with salt and pepper.

3 Evenly sprinkle half the cheeses on the dough. Top with half each of the ham and tomatoes, if using.

4 Shake the peel lightly and slide the flatbread onto the hot baking stone. Bake until browned, 6 to 7 minutes (10 to 14 minutes for gluten-free crusts).

5 Transfer the flatbread to a firm surface and cut it into slices. Serve immediately, garnished with mustard aioli, if desired.

6 Repeat all the steps using the second dough round.

BARBECUED CHICKEN PIZZA

There are many variations of this famous (or is it infamous?) pizza. This is my version, which uses my roasted red onions and whatever leftover chicken you have on hand. Try replacing the barbecue sauce with 3 to 4 tablespoons of hoisin for an interesting Asian-inspired twist. Or even swap the chicken for duck!

2 pizza rounds of your choice

All-purpose flour for sprinkling

2 teaspoons extra-virgin olive oil

½ teaspoon minced garlic

¼ cup barbecue sauce

⅔ cup Roasted Red Onions (see page 37)

½ pound cooked boneless, skinless chicken (any combination of light and dark meat), pulled into bite-size pieces

6 ounces Gouda cheese, shredded

2 tablespoons chopped scallion greens, for garnish

Kosher salt and freshly ground black pepper

1 One hour before baking, place a baking stone in the oven and preheat it to 500°F (450°F for gluten-free crusts).

2 Roll out 1 pizza round as thinly as possible and place it on a pizza peel sprinkled with flour. Leaving an outer lip all around the edge of the dough, cover the surface with half the oil and garlic; season with salt and pepper.

3 Evenly spread half the barbecue sauce on the dough. Top with half each of the onions, chicken, and Gouda.

4 Shake the peel lightly and slide the pizza onto the hot baking stone. Bake until browned, 6 to 7 minutes (10 to 14 minutes for gluten-free crusts).

5 Transfer the pizza to a firm surface and cut it into slices. Serve immediately, garnished with half the scallion greens.

6 Repeat all the steps using the second dough round.

KALE AND CHORIZO PIZZA

Kale and pork are a natural combination, and long before kale became trendy, the Spanish were using it in *caldo gallego*, a traditional white bean soup with kale and chorizo. The kale is cooked long and slow and melts in your mouth. Here, with a nod to with sliced chorizo.

2 pizza rounds of your choice

All-purpose flour for sprinkling

2 teaspoons extra-virgin olive oil

½ teaspoon minced garlic

½ to ¾ cup Sautéed Kale (see page 51), chopped

2 boiled or roasted red new or Yukon gold potatoes, thinly sliced (optional)

4 ounces mozzarella cheese, shredded

4 ounces dried Spanish chorizo, thinly sliced

¼ cup sliced roasted red pepper from a jar (optional)

2 tablespoons freshly grated Pecorino Romano cheese

1 tablespoon chopped fresh parsley, for garnish

Kosher salt and freshly ground black pepper

1 One hour before baking, place a baking stone in the oven and preheat it to 500°F (450°F for gluten-free crusts).

2 Roll out 1 pizza round as thinly as possible and place it on a pizza peel sprinkled with flour. Leaving an outer lip all around the edge of the dough, cover the surface with half the oil and garlic; season with salt and pepper.

3 Evenly distribute half each of the kale and potatoes, if using, on the dough. Top with half each of the mozzarella, chorizo, red pepper, if using, and Pecorino Romano.

4 Shake the peel lightly and slide the pizza onto the hot baking stone. Bake until browned, 6 to 7 minutes (10 to 14 minutes for gluten-free crusts).

5 Transfer the pizza to a firm surface and cut it into slices. Serve immediately, garnished with half the parsley.

6 Repeat all the steps using the second dough round.

SALUMI PIZZA

Salumi is the Italian word for "cured meats," and this pizza has got them in spades. Other options include prosciutto, pancetta, guanciale, and speck—the only limit is your imagination.

2 pizza rounds of your choice

All-purpose flour for sprinkling

2 teaspoons extra-virgin olive oil

½ teaspoon minced garlic

⅔ cup Marinara Sauce (see page 16)

5 ounces fresh mozzarella cheese, torn into small pieces

3 ounces Provolone cheese, shredded

1 ounce capocollo (Italian pork cold cut), thinly sliced

1 ounce salami, thinly sliced

1 ounce mortadella (Italian sausage), thinly sliced

2 pickled cherry peppers, thinly sliced, for garnish

¼ red onion, peeled and thinly sliced, for garnish

Kosher salt and freshly ground black pepper

1 One hour before baking, place a baking stone in the oven and preheat it to 500°F (450°F for gluten-free crusts).

2 Roll out 1 pizza round as thinly as possible and place it on a pizza peel sprinkled with flour. Leaving an outer lip all around the edge of the dough, cover the surface with half the oil and garlic; season with salt and pepper.

3 Evenly spread half the sauce on the dough. Top with half each of the cheeses and the meats.

4 Shake the peel lightly and slide the pizza onto the hot baking stone. Bake until browned, 6 to 7 minutes (10 to 14 minutes for gluten-free crusts).

5 Transfer the pizza to a firm surface and cut it into slices. Serve immediately, garnished with half the peppers and onions.

6 Repeat all the steps using the second dough round.

TRES CARNES FLATBREAD

Not to be outdone by the Salumi Pizza, Tres Carnes takes the best of Spanish *charcutería* and puts it on a flatbread with melted Manchego cheese and Spanish olives. *¡Delicioso!*

2 pizza rounds of your choice

All-purpose flour for sprinkling

½ teaspoon minced garlic

3 to 4 ounces Manchego cheese, thinly sliced

1 ounce dried Spanish chorizo, thinly sliced

1 ounce lomo (cured pork loin), thinly sliced

⅓ cup sliced green Spanish olives

1 ounce Cabrales (Spanish blue) cheese, crumbled (optional)

¼ cup sliced roasted red peppers (optional)

2 ounces Jamón Serrano or Ibérico ham, very thinly sliced

Kosher salt and freshly ground black pepper

1 One hour before baking, place a baking stone in the oven and preheat it to 500°F (450°F for gluten-free crusts).

2 Roll out 1 pizza round as thinly as possible and place it on a pizza peel sprinkled with flour. Leaving an outer lip all around the edge of the dough, cover the surface with half the garlic; season with salt and pepper.

3 Evenly distribute half the Manchego slices on the dough. Top with half each of the chorizo, lomo, olives, and red peppers, if using.

4 Shake the peel lightly and slide the flatbread onto the hot baking stone. Bake until browned, 6 to 7 minutes (10 to 14 minutes for gluten-free crusts).

5 Transfer the flatbread to a firm surface, drape it immediately with half the Jamón Serrano slices, and cut it into slices. Serve immediately.

6 Repeat all the steps using the second dough round.

ITALIAN SAUSAGE AND RICOTTA PIZZA

A basic sausage pie becomes something extra special when dolloped with herbed ricotta.

2 pizza rounds of your choice

All-purpose flour for sprinkling

2 teaspoons extra-virgin olive oil

½ teaspoon minced garlic

1 cup Marinara Sauce (see page 16) or Roasted Tomato Sauce (see page 17)

5 ounces mozzarella cheese, shredded

8 ounces (about 2 links) sweet or hot Italian sausage, cooked and thinly sliced or crumbled

¼ red onion, peeled and thinly sliced

⅓ cup Herbed Ricotta Cheese (see page 41) (or use plain ricotta cheese)

2 teaspoons freshly grated Parmesan cheese

Kosher salt and freshly ground black pepper

1 One hour before baking, place a baking stone in the oven and preheat it to 500°F (450°F for gluten-free crusts).

2 Roll out 1 pizza round as thinly as possible and place it on a pizza peel sprinkled with flour. Leaving an outer lip all around the edge of the dough, cover the surface with half the oil and garlic; season with salt and pepper.

3 Evenly spread half the sauce on the dough. Top with half each of the mozzarella, sausage, and onion. Dot with half the ricotta and sprinkle with half the Parmesan.

4 Shake the peel lightly and slide the pizza onto the hot baking stone. Bake until browned, 6 to 7 minutes (10 to 14 minutes for gluten-free crusts).

5 Transfer the pizza to a firm surface and cut it into slices. Serve immediately, garnished with half the remaining onion.

6 Repeat all the steps using the second dough round.

ROASTED GARLIC, CHICKEN, AND RED PEPPER PIZZA

A whole head of garlic for two pizzas may sound like a lot, but it's just the right amount when it's nutty and mild roasted garlic. The garlicky base is topped with roast chicken and smothered in Cheddar and mozzarella cheeses. Bell pepper and basil provide a fresh contrast.

2 pizza rounds of your choice

All-purpose flour for sprinkling

2 teaspoons extra-virgin olive oil

1 head Roasted Garlic (see page 36), cloves squeezed from their skins and coarsely chopped

½ pound cooked boneless, skinless chicken (any combination of light and dark meat), pulled into bite-size pieces

3 ounces Cheddar cheese, shredded

3 ounces mozzarella cheese, shredded

½ red bell pepper, seeded and thinly sliced

2 tablespoons chopped fresh basil or parsley leaves, for garnish

Kosher salt and freshly ground black pepper

1 One hour before baking, place a baking stone in the oven and preheat it to 500°F (450°F for gluten-free crusts).

2 Roll out 1 pizza round as thinly as possible and place it on a pizza peel sprinkled with flour. Leaving an outer lip all around the edge of the dough, cover the surface with half the oil; season with salt and pepper.

3 Evenly distribute half each of the roasted garlic and chicken on the dough. Top with half each of the cheeses and bell pepper.

4 Shake the peel lightly and slide the pizza onto the hot baking stone. Bake until browned, 6 to 7 minutes (10 to 14 minutes for gluten-free crusts).

5 Transfer the pizza to a firm surface and cut it into slices. Serve immediately, garnished with half the basil.

6 Repeat all the steps using the second dough round.

BACON AND CHEDDAR FLATBREAD

As a late-night snack, a quick lunch, or even dinner (hey, you've got your salad greens right there!), Bacon and Cheddar Flatbread is definitely crave-worthy.

2 pizza rounds of your choice

All-purpose flour for sprinkling

2 teaspoons extra-virgin olive oil, plus extra for drizzling

½ teaspoon minced garlic

6 ounces Cheddar cheese, shredded

3 slices thick-cut bacon, cut into ¼-inch-long narrow strips ("lardons") and cooked

2 plum tomatoes, thinly sliced and seeded

2 cups baby arugula (about 2½ ounces) (optional), for serving

Lemon wedges, for serving

Kosher salt and freshly ground black pepper

1 One hour before baking, place a baking stone in the oven and preheat it to 500°F (450°F for gluten-free crusts).

2 Roll out 1 pizza round as thinly as possible and place it on a pizza peel sprinkled with flour. Leaving an outer lip all around the edge of the dough, cover the surface with half the oil and garlic; season with salt and pepper.

3 Evenly distribute half the Cheddar, lardons, and tomatoes on the dough.

4 Shake the peel lightly and slide the flatbread onto the hot baking stone. Bake until browned, 6 to 7 minutes (10 to 14 minutes for gluten-free crusts).

5 Transfer the flatbread to a firm surface, top with half the arugula, if desired, a drizzle of olive oil, and a squeeze of one lemon wedge. Cut it into slices and serve immediately.

6 Repeat all the steps using the second dough round.

CHEESESTEAK PIZZA

I make no claims to cheesesteak authenticity here (do you hear me, Philly?), but this sure tastes good with a cold beer. The secret to slicing the steak thinly enough is to freeze it for at least 30 minutes before even attempting to slice it.

½ pound rib eye or skirt steak

1 teaspoon olive oil

½ yellow onion, peeled and thinly sliced

½ green bell pepper, seeded and thinly sliced

2 pizza rounds of your choice

All-purpose flour for sprinkling

2 teaspoons extra-virgin olive oil

½ teaspoon minced garlic

6 ounces Provolone cheese, thinly sliced

⅔ cup Marinara Sauce (see page 16) (optional)

Kosher salt and freshly ground black pepper

1 One hour before baking, place a baking stone in the oven and preheat it to 500°F (450°F for gluten-free crusts). To make the steak easier to slice, place it in the freezer for at least 30 minutes to firm up.

2 Slice the steak as thinly as possible (the thinner the better). In a large skillet over medium-high heat, heat the oil until hot. Add the steak and cook until browned on both sides. Remove the steak from the pan and set aside. Add the onion and bell pepper and cook, stirring occasionally, until softened, 8 to 10 minutes.

3 Roll out 1 pizza round as thinly as possible and place it on a pizza peel sprinkled with flour. Leaving an outer lip all around the edge of the dough, cover the surface with half the oil and garlic; season with salt and pepper.

4 Evenly distribute half each of the Provolone, steak, and onion mixture on the dough. Drizzle with half the sauce, if using.

5 Shake the peel lightly and slide the pizza onto the hot baking stone. Bake until browned, 6 to 7 minutes (10 to 14 minutes for gluten-free crusts).

6 Transfer the pizza to a firm surface and cut it into slices. Serve immediately.

7 Repeat all the steps (except step 2) using the second dough round.

PEPPERONI, RED ONION, AND OLIVE PIZZA

Make sure you use a high-quality, oil-cured olive here, like the kind you get from the olive bar at the supermarket, not canned black olives. You can substitute salami for the pepperoni, if you wish.

2 pizza rounds of your choice

All-purpose flour for sprinkling

2 teaspoons extra-virgin olive oil

½ teaspoon minced garlic

1 cup Roasted Tomato Sauce (see page 17)

8 ounces mozzarella cheese, shredded

4 ounces pepperoni, thinly sliced

½ red onion, peeled and thinly sliced

½ cup sliced green or black oil-cured olives (such as Manzanilla, Niçoise, or Kalamata)

2 tablespoons freshly grated Pecorino Romano cheese

Kosher salt and freshly ground black pepper

1 One hour before baking, place a baking stone in the oven and preheat it to 500°F (450°F for gluten-free crusts).

2 Roll out 1 pizza round as thinly as possible and place it on a pizza peel sprinkled with flour. Leaving an outer lip all around the edge of the dough, cover the surface with half the oil and garlic; season with salt and pepper.

3 Evenly spread half the sauce on the dough. Top with half each of the mozzarella, pepperoni, onion, and olives. Sprinkle with half the Pecorino Romano.

4 Shake the peel lightly and slide the pizza onto the hot baking stone. Bake until browned, 6 to 7 minutes (10 to 14 minutes for gluten-free crusts).

5 Transfer the pizza to a firm surface and cut it into slices. Serve immediately.

6 Repeat all the steps using the second dough round.

AMATRICIANA

This pizza was inspired by Amatriciana, the spicy Italian pasta sauce made with guanciale (or with the easier-to-find pancetta), onions, tomato, and hot pepper.

2 pizza rounds of your choice

All-purpose flour for sprinkling

2 teaspoons extra-virgin olive oil

½ teaspoon minced garlic

⅔ cup Marinara Sauce (see page 16)

½ cup Caramelized Onions (see page 38)

½ teaspoon red pepper flakes

2 tablespoons grated Pecorino

Romano cheese

3 ounces Fontina cheese, shredded

3 ounces mozzarella cheese, shredded

4 ounces pancetta, diced and cooked until brown

2 teaspoons chopped fresh parsley (optional)

Kosher salt and freshly ground black pepper

1 One hour before baking, place a baking stone in the oven and preheat it to 500°F (450°F for gluten-free crusts).

2 Roll out 1 pizza round as thinly as possible and place it on a pizza peel sprinkled with flour. Leaving an outer lip all around the edge of the dough, cover the surface with half the oil and garlic; season with salt and pepper.

3 Evenly spread half the sauce on the dough. Top with half the onions. Sprinkle with half the pepper flakes, then top with half each of the cheeses and pancetta.

4 Shake the peel lightly and slide the pizza onto the hot baking stone. Bake until browned, 6 to 7 minutes (10 to 14 minutes for gluten-free crusts).

5 Transfer the pizza to a firm surface and cut it into slices. Serve immediately, garnished with half the parsley, if using.

6 Repeat all the steps using the second dough round.

CREAMY CHICKEN WITH HERBS PIZZA

Creamy cheese, delicate herbs, and garlic béchamel make the perfect canvas for this chicken pizza.

2 pizza rounds of your choice

All-purpose flour for sprinkling

⅔ cup Roasted Garlic Béchamel (see page 25)

½ pound cooked boneless, skinless chicken (any combination of light and dark meat), pulled into bite-size pieces

6 ounces creamy-style cheese (such as Fontina, Havarti, or Gouda)

2 teaspoons chopped fresh parsley

2 teaspoons chopped fresh tarragon

2 teaspoons chopped fresh chives

Kosher salt and freshly ground black pepper

1 One hour before baking, place a baking stone in the oven and preheat it to 500°F (450°F for gluten-free crusts).

2 Roll out 1 pizza round as thinly as possible and place it on a pizza peel sprinkled with flour. Leaving an outer lip all around the edge of the dough, season the surface with salt and pepper.

3 Evenly spread half the béchamel on the dough. Top with half each of the chicken and cheese.

4 Shake the peel lightly and slide the pizza onto the hot baking stone. Bake until browned, 6 to 7 minutes (10 to 14 minutes for gluten-free crusts).

5 Transfer the pizza to a firm surface and garnish it with half the herbs. Let rest 1 or 2 minutes to allow the heat of the pizza to gently warm and wilt the herbs. Cut it into slices and serve immediately.

6 Repeat all the steps using the second dough round.

TURKISH-STYLE FLATBREAD WITH HERBS, TOMATO, AND SUMAC ONIONS

Lahmacun is a Turkish flatbread topped with spiced lamb or beef. My version takes a bit of time to assemble, but the flavor explosion you'll experience when you taste it will make it all worth it. The freshness of the herbs, onions, and tomatoes contrasts brilliantly with the strongly spiced meat. All of this is topped off with a cooling herbed yogurt sauce.

A FEW TIPS: Aleppo pepper is a relatively mild pepper, ground a little coarser than cayenne pepper. If you can't find it, use the smaller quantity of cayenne. Sumac is a spice with a citrusy flavor that's very traditional in Middle Eastern dishes, but a little lemon juice can be used in its place. Finally, if your beef or lamb is very fatty, even if you drain it well after cooking, it may continue to give off fat in the oven so you may wish to place your pizza on a lipped pizza pan on top of the baking stone to avoid spills.

½ teaspoon ground cumin

½ teaspoon paprika

¼ teaspoon ground coriander

½ teaspoon Aleppo pepper, or ¼ teaspoon cayenne pepper

¼ teaspoon plus 1 pinch ground sumac, or 1 teaspoon freshly squeezed lemon juice

Pinch cinnamon

½ teaspoon salt

½ yellow onion, peeled and minced, plus ¼ yellow onion, peeled and thinly sliced

½ pound ground lamb or beef

1 clove garlic, minced

½ jalapeño pepper, seeded and minced (optional)

1 teaspoon tomato paste

3 plum tomatoes, seeded, cored, and diced

3 tablespoons chopped fresh parsley

2 tablespoons chopped fresh mint (or more parsley)

2 pizza rounds of your choice

All-purpose flour for sprinkling

Herbed Yogurt Sauce (see page 32), for garnish

Kosher salt and freshly ground black pepper

1 One hour before baking, place a baking stone in the oven and preheat it to 500°F (450°F for gluten-free crusts).

2 In a small bowl, stir together the cumin, paprika, coriander, Aleppo pepper, ¼ teaspoon of the sumac, cinnamon, and salt. Set aside.

3 In a separate small bowl, toss the sliced onion with a pinch of ground sumac.

4 In a medium skillet over medium heat, cook the lamb until it is no longer pink; drain and transfer it to a plate to rest. Drain all but 1 teaspoon of the fat from the pan, then add the minced onions. Cook until softened, 5 to 6 minutes. Stir in the garlic and jalapeño, if using, and cook until they are fragrant, about 30 seconds. Add the tomato paste and 1 tomato and stir until fully combined. Add the reserved spice mixture and cook, stirring, until fragrant, 30 to 60 seconds. Return the meat to the pan and stir until fully combined; the mixture should be fairly dry. Remove the pan from the heat and stir in 2 tablespoons of the parsley and 1 tablespoon of the mint. Set aside while you prepare the dough.

5 Roll out 1 pizza round as thinly as possible and place it on a pizza peel sprinkled with flour. Leaving an outer lip all around the edge of the dough, season the surface with salt and pepper.

6 Evenly spread half the meat mixture on the dough. Shake the peel lightly and slide the pizza onto the hot baking stone. Bake until browned, 6 to 7 minutes (10 to 14 minutes for gluten-free crusts).

7 Transfer the pizza to a firm surface and garnish it with half the remaining herbs, 1 diced plum tomato, half the sumac onions, and a drizzle of yogurt sauce. Cut it into slices and serve immediately.

8 Repeat all the steps (except steps 2, 3, and 4) using the second dough round.

CHORIZO, POBLANO, AND COTIJA PIZZA

Cotija is a salty, often crumbly Mexican cheese that's delicious when paired with other Mexican flavors like fresh chorizo and poblano pepper. If you can't find Cotija, you can substitute queso blanco or queso fresco. If you have the time, roast the poblano instead of sautéing it for a more complex and smoky flavor. Place it under the broiler until it blackens in spots, or blacken it over the flame of a gas stove, turning it occasionally with tongs (don't walk away from it!). Put the blackened pepper in a bowl, cover it with plastic wrap, and let it cool. When it's cool enough to handle, peel, seed, and slice it.

2 teaspoons extra-virgin olive oil

1 poblano pepper, seeded and thinly sliced

½ onion, peeled and thinly sliced

½ teaspoon minced garlic

2 pizza rounds of your choice

All-purpose flour for sprinkling

1 cup chopped Roasted Tomatoes (see page 42), drained

4 ounces mozzarella cheese, shredded

2 ounces Cotija cheese, crumbled

6 ounces Mexican-style fresh chorizo, cooked and crumbled

A few fresh cilantro leaves, torn, for garnish

Kosher salt and freshly ground black pepper

1 One hour before baking, place a baking stone in the oven and preheat it to 500°F (450°F for gluten-free crusts).

2 In a medium skillet over medium-high heat, heat the oil until hot then add the poblano and onion. Sauté, stirring occasionally, until starting to brown, 5 to 7 minutes. Add the garlic and cook until fragrant, about 30 seconds. Season with salt and pepper. Set aside to cool.

3 Roll out 1 pizza round as thinly as possible and place it on a pizza peel sprinkled with flour. Leaving an outer lip all around the edge of the dough, cover the surface with half each of the remaining oil and the minced garlic; season with salt and pepper.

4 Evenly distribute half each of the tomatoes, mozzarella, Cotija, chorizo, and poblano mixture on the dough.

5 Shake the peel lightly and slide the pizza onto the hot baking stone. Bake until browned, 6 to 7 minutes (10 to 14 minutes for gluten-free crusts).

6 Transfer the pizza to a firm surface, garnish it with a few torn cilantro leaves, and cut it into slices. Serve immediately.

7 Repeat all the steps (except step 2) using the second dough round.

BLACKENED BRUSSELS SPROUTS, BACON, AND PROVOLONE PIZZA

Brussels sprouts and bacon are a match made in heaven. There's just something about the salty, fatty, smoky goodness of bacon that goes well with any cabbage-like vegetable—not to mention countless other foods. Sophisticated, yet utterly satisfying.

2 pizza rounds of your choice

All-purpose flour for sprinkling

2 teaspoons extra-virgin olive oil

½ teaspoon minced garlic

6 ounces Provolone cheese, shredded

3 slices thick-cut bacon, cooked and crumbled

½ pound Blackened Brussels Sprouts (see page 62)

2 tablespoons freshly grated Parmesan cheese

Kosher salt and freshly ground black pepper

1 One hour before baking, place a baking stone in the oven and preheat it to 500°F (450°F for gluten-free crusts).

2 Roll out 1 pizza round as thinly as possible and place it on a pizza peel sprinkled with flour. Leaving an outer lip all around the edge of the dough, cover the surface with half the oil and garlic; season with salt and pepper.

3 Top the dough with half the bacon. Evenly sprinkle half the Provolone, then top with half the Brussels sprouts and Parmesan.

4 Shake the peel lightly and slide the pizza onto the hot baking stone. Bake until browned, 6 to 7 minutes (10 to 14 minutes for gluten-free crusts).

5 Transfer the pizza to a firm surface and cut it into slices. Serve immediately.

6 Repeat all the steps using the second dough round.

RICOTTA, SPECK, AND MUSHROOM PIZZA

If you haven't tried speck, or smoked prosciutto, you're missing out. Pair it with ricotta and sautéed mushrooms for a delicious treat.

2 pizza rounds of your choice

All-purpose flour for sprinkling

2 teaspoons extra-virgin olive oil

½ teaspoon minced garlic

4 ounces mozzarella cheese, thinly sliced

3 ounces speck, thinly sliced

½ cup Sautéed Mushrooms (see page 49)

¼ cup ricotta cheese

Kosher salt and freshly ground
   black pepper

1 One hour before baking, place a baking stone in the oven and preheat it to 500°F (450°F for gluten-free crusts).

2 Roll out 1 pizza round as thinly as possible and place it on a pizza peel sprinkled with flour. Leaving an outer lip all around the edge of the dough, cover the surface with half the oil and garlic; season with salt and pepper.

3 Evenly sprinkle half the mozzarella on the dough. Top with half each of the speck and mushrooms and dot with half the ricotta.

4 Shake the peel lightly and slide the pizza onto the hot baking stone. Bake until browned, 6 to 7 minutes (10 to 14 minutes for gluten-free crusts).

5 Transfer the pizza to a firm surface and cut it into slices. Serve immediately.

6 Repeat all the steps using the second dough round.

SPECK, PEAR, AND WALNUT GORGONZOLA PIZZA

This pizza may seem on the adventurous side, but the smokiness of the speck goes really well with delicate roasted pears and rich walnut Gorgonzola.

2 pizza rounds of your choice

All-purpose flour for sprinkling

2 teaspoons extra-virgin olive oil

4 ounces mozzarella cheese, thinly sliced

3 ounces speck, thinly sliced

1 Roasted Pear (see page 48), thinly sliced

¼ cup Walnut Gorgonzola (see page 44)

Kosher salt and freshly ground black pepper

1 One hour before baking, place a baking stone in the oven and preheat it to 500°F (450°F for gluten-free crusts).

2 Roll out 1 pizza round as thinly as possible and place it on a pizza peel sprinkled with flour. Leaving an outer lip all around the edge of the dough, cover the surface with half the oil; season with salt and pepper.

3 Evenly sprinkle half the mozzarella on the dough. Top with half each of the speck and pear and dot with half the walnut Gorgonzola.

4 Shake the peel lightly and slide the pizza onto the hot baking stone. Bake until browned, 6 to 7 minutes (10 to 14 minutes for gluten-free crusts).

5 Transfer the pizza to a firm surface and cut it into slices. Serve immediately.

6 Repeat all the steps using the second dough round.

BUTTERNUT SQUASH, PANCETTA, RICOTTA, AND RED ONION PIZZA

Heaven is this pizza, topped with sweet roasted butternut squash, crispy pancetta cubes, creamy ricotta, and crunchy red onion.

2 pizza rounds of your choice

All-purpose flour for sprinkling

2 teaspoons extra-virgin olive oil

½ teaspoon minced garlic

4 ounces mozzarella cheese, shredded

3 ounces pancetta, cubed and browned

1½ cups Roasted Butternut Squash (see page 39)

¼ cup ricotta cheese

½ red onion, peeled and thinly sliced

Kosher salt and freshly ground black pepper

1 One hour before baking, place a baking stone in the oven and preheat it to 500°F (450°F for gluten-free crusts).

2 Roll out 1 pizza round as thinly as possible and place it on a pizza peel sprinkled with flour. Leaving an outer lip all around the edge of the dough, cover the surface with half the oil and garlic; season with salt and pepper.

3 Evenly sprinkle half the mozzarella on the dough. Top with half each of the pancetta, squash, ricotta, and onion.

4 Shake the peel lightly and slide the pizza onto the hot baking stone. Bake until browned, 6 to 7 minutes (10 to 14 minutes for gluten-free crusts).

5 Transfer the pizza to a firm surface and cut it into slices. Serve immediately.

6 Repeat all the steps using the second dough round.

CHICKEN TIKKA MASALA NAAN PIZZA

A perennial favorite at Indian restaurants, chicken tikka masala is rich and spicy, with tender chunks of chicken simmered in a yogurt- or cream-based sauce. My Chicken Tikka Masala Naan Pizza, made with tikka masala simmer sauce from a jar and cooked chicken, is a quick weeknight meal that can satisfy that Indian-food craving almost as fast as delivery!

2 large rounds prepared naan bread (about 8 to 10 inches in diameter)

½ pound cooked boneless, skinless chicken (any combination of light and dark meat), pulled into bite-size pieces

½ cup plus 2 tablespoons tikka masala simmer sauce from a jar

5 ounces mozzarella cheese, shredded

2 plum tomatoes, thinly sliced and seeded

¼ red onion, peeled and thinly sliced

1 tablespoon chopped fresh cilantro leaves, for garnish

Plain yogurt or Herbed Yogurt Sauce (see page 32), for serving (optional)

1 Preheat the oven to 450°F.

2 Place the rounds of naan on a half sheet pan.

3 In a small bowl, toss the chicken with 2 tablespoons of the simmer sauce. Evenly divide the remaining sauce over the naan rounds. Top with the chicken mixture, mozzarella, tomatoes, and onion. Bake until browned, 8 to 10 minutes.

4 Transfer the pizzas to a firm surface and cut them into slices. Serve immediately, garnished with the cilantro and yogurt, if desired.

RADICCHIO AND PANCETTA PIZZA

Radicchio's mild bitterness is tempered by the salty, meaty burst of pancetta on this perfectly balanced pizza.

2 pizza rounds of your choice

All-purpose flour for sprinkling

2 teaspoons extra-virgin olive oil

½ teaspoon minced garlic

⅔ cup Marinara Sauce (16) or Roasted Tomato Sauce (see page 17)

8 ounces mozzarella cheese, shredded

1½ cups thinly sliced radicchio

3 ounces pancetta, cubed and cooked

2 tablespoons freshly grated Parmesan cheese

Kosher salt and freshly ground black pepper

1 One hour before baking, place a baking stone in the oven and preheat it to 500°F (450°F for gluten-free crusts).

2 Roll out 1 pizza round as thinly as possible and place it on a pizza peel sprinkled with flour. Leaving an outer lip all around the edge of the dough, cover the surface with half the oil and garlic; season with salt and pepper.

3 Evenly spread half the sauce on the dough. Top with half each of the mozzarella, radicchio, pancetta, and Parmesan.

4 Shake the peel lightly and slide the pizza onto the hot baking stone. Bake until browned, 6 to 7 minutes (10 to 14 minutes for gluten-free crusts).

5 Transfer the pizza to a firm surface and cut it into slices. Serve immediately.

6 Repeat all the steps using the second dough round.

SMOKED MOZZARELLA, SALAMI, AND BLACK OLIVES PIZZA

Here the ingredients do all of the heavy lifting for you. You just need to assemble them. Choose a good quality Italian salami, oil-cured olives (no canned here, please!), and the best smoked mozzarella you can find.

2 pizza rounds of your choice

All-purpose flour for sprinkling

2 teaspoons extra-virgin olive oil

½ teaspoon minced garlic

⅔ cup Roasted Tomato Sauce (see page 17)

8 ounces smoked mozzarella cheese, shredded

3 ounces salami, thinly sliced

¼ cup sliced oil-cured black olives (such as Kalamata)

Kosher salt and freshly ground black pepper

1 One hour before baking, place a baking stone in the oven and preheat it to 500°F (450°F for gluten-free crusts).

2 Roll out 1 pizza round as thinly as possible and place it on a pizza peel sprinkled with flour. Leaving an outer lip all around the edge of the dough, cover the surface with half the oil and garlic; season with salt and pepper.

3 Evenly spread half the sauce on the dough. Top with half each of the mozzarella, salami and olives.

4 Shake the peel lightly and slide the pizza onto the hot baking stone. Bake until browned, 6 to 7 minutes (10 to 14 minutes for gluten-free crusts).

5 Transfer the pizza to a firm surface and cut it into slices. Serve immediately.

6 Repeat all the steps using the second dough round.

MEXICAN CHORIZO, POTATO, AND FENNEL PIZZA

Chorizo and potato are a tasty and comforting combination often used in tacos. Here, they pair up with a roasted tomato sauce and fennel for a knockout pizza.

2 pizza rounds of your choice

All-purpose flour for sprinkling

2 teaspoons extra-virgin olive oil

½ teaspoon minced garlic

⅔ cup Roasted Tomato Sauce (see page 17)

6 ounces mozzarella cheese or *queso quesadilla,* shredded

6 ounces Mexican-style fresh chorizo, cooked and crumbled

2 boiled or roasted red new or Yukon gold potatoes, thinly sliced

½ bulb fennel, thinly sliced (optional)

Fresh cilantro leaves, for garnish

Kosher salt and freshly ground black pepper

1 One hour before baking, place a baking stone in the oven and preheat it to 500°F (450°F for gluten-free crusts).

2 Roll out 1 pizza round as thinly as possible and place it on a pizza peel sprinkled with flour. Leaving an outer lip all around the edge of the dough, cover the surface with half the oil and garlic; season with salt and pepper.

3 Evenly spread half the sauce on the dough. Top with half each of the mozzarella, chorizo, potato slices, and fennel.

4 Shake the peel lightly and slide the pizza onto the hot baking stone. Bake until browned, 6 to 7 minutes (10 to 14 minutes for gluten-free crusts).

5 Transfer the pizza to a firm surface, garnish it with torn cilantro leaves, and cut it into slices. Serve immediately.

6 Repeat all the steps using the second dough round.

6

SEAFOOD PIZZAS

Seafood dishes are perennial favorites, and in many cultures around the world seafood is prized. The most common fish topping on pizza is, of course, the love-it-or-hate-it anchovy, but shrimp, scallops, and other delicacies of the sea can make pizza a real luxurious treat.

WHITE CLAM PIZZA

With fresh oregano, white clam pizza is a briny and simply delicious pizza. The hardest part, I'll admit, is shucking the clams. Discard any clams with broken shells or those that don't close when you tap on them. Also, leave a good lip on the edge of this pizza to accommodate the clam "liquor" (the liquid from the opened and cooked clams). To avoid spillage on the baking stone, consider using a thin pizza pan.

18 to 24 littleneck clams, well washed, shucked, and very roughly chopped, including the clam liquor, or 1 (6.5-ounce) can clams, lightly drained

2 tablespoons extra-virgin olive oil

4 teaspoons roughly chopped fresh oregano leaves

2 pizza rounds of your choice

All-purpose flour for sprinkling

½ teaspoon minced garlic

3 tablespoons freshly grated Parmesan cheese

Kosher salt and freshly ground black pepper

1 One hour before baking, place a baking stone in the oven and preheat it to 500°F (450°F for gluten-free crusts).

2 At the same time, in a small bowl, stir together the clams and their liquor, the oil, and 1 teaspoon of the oregano. Set aside.

3 Roll out 1 pizza round as thinly as possible and place it on a pizza peel sprinkled with flour. Leaving an outer lip all around the edge of the dough, cover the surface with half the garlic; season with salt and pepper.

4 Evenly spread half the clam mixture (including the liquid) on the dough. Top with 1 teaspoon of the oregano and sprinkle with 1 tablespoon of the Parmesan.

5 Shake the peel lightly and slide the pizza onto the hot baking stone. Bake until browned, 6 to 7 minutes (10 to 14 minutes for gluten-free crusts).

6 Transfer the pizza to a firm surface and cut it into slices. Serve immediately, garnished with ½ teaspoon of the oregano, and 1½ teaspoons of the Parmesan.

7 Repeat all the steps (except 2) using the second dough round.

SHRIMP AND CHORIZO PIZZA

Shrimp and Chorizo Pizza is smoky and rich with roasted flavors from the piquillo peppers and tomato sauce.

2 pizza rounds of your choice

All-purpose flour for sprinkling

2 teaspoons extra-virgin olive oil

½ teaspoon minced garlic

1 cup Roasted Tomato Sauce (see page 17) or Marinara Sauce (see page 16)

4 ounces mozzarella cheese, shredded

5 ounces dried Spanish chorizo, thinly sliced

9 to 10 large shrimp (21-25 count), peeled, deveined, and sliced lengthwise

¼ cup sliced piquillo or roasted red peppers from a jar

2 tablespoons freshly grated Parmesan cheese

1 tablespoon chopped fresh parsley or cilantro, for garnish

Kosher salt and freshly ground black pepper

1 One hour before baking, place a baking stone in the oven and preheat it to 500°F (450°F for gluten-free crusts).

2 Roll out 1 pizza round as thinly as possible and place it on a pizza peel sprinkled with flour. Leaving an outer lip all around the edge of the dough, cover the surface with half the garlic; season with salt and pepper.

3 Evenly spread half the sauce over crust. Top with the half each of the mozzarella, chorizo, shrimp, and peppers. Sprinkle with half the Parmesan.

4 Shake the peel lightly and slide the pizza onto the hot baking stone. Bake until golden brown, 6 to 7 minutes (10 to 14 minutes for gluten-free crusts).

5 Transfer the pizza to a firm surface and cut it into slices. Serve immediately, garnished with half the parsley.

6 Repeat all the steps using the second dough round.

SPICY SHRIMP AND LEEKS PIZZA

If you like shrimp fra diavolo, you'll love this spicy shrimp pizza topped with delicious caramelized leeks and dollops of ricotta cheese.

1½ tablespoons unsalted butter

2 teaspoons extra-virgin olive oil

5-6 leeks, washed and julienned

2 pizza rounds of your choice

All-purpose flour for sprinkling

½ teaspoon minced garlic

1 hot pepper (jalapeño, serrano, or cherry), seeded and finely minced, or 1 teaspoon red pepper flakes

9 to 10 large shrimp (21-25 count), peeled, deveined, and sliced lengthwise

1 cup Marinara Sauce (see page 16)

⅓ cup ricotta cheese

6 scallions, thinly sliced lengthwise, for garnish

Kosher salt and freshly ground black pepper

1 One hour before baking, place a baking stone in the oven and preheat it to 500°F (450°F for gluten-free crusts).

2 Place the butter and oil in a large skillet over medium heat. When the butter has melted, reduce heat to low, add the leeks, and stir. Cook, stirring regularly, until they are lightly browned, about 30 minutes.

3 Roll out 1 pizza round as thinly as possible and place it on a pizza peel sprinkled with flour. Leaving an outer lip all around the edge of the dough, cover the surface with 1 tablespoon oil, half the garlic; season with salt and pepper.

4 In a small bowl, combine the hot pepper and shrimp, being sure the pepper evenly coats the shrimp.

5 Evenly spread half the sauce on the dough. Top with half each of the caramelized leeks and the shrimp mixture. Dot with half the ricotta.

6 Shake the peel lightly and slide the pizza onto the hot baking stone. Bake until browned, 6 to 7 minutes (10 to 14 minutes for gluten-free crusts).

7 Transfer the pizza to a firm surface and cut it into slices. Serve immediately.

8 Repeat steps 3 and 5-8 using the second dough round.

SHRIMP, FONTINA, AND PESTO PIZZA

Rich and delicious, this pizza hits all the right notes. If you don't have Fontina, you can substitute Gouda or Provolone, or just use all mozzarella.

2 pizza rounds of your choice

All-purpose flour for sprinkling

2 teaspoons extra-virgin olive oil

½ teaspoon minced garlic

⅓ cup Traditional Basil Pesto (see page 23) or pesto sauce from a jar

¼ cup shredded mozzarella cheese

¼ cup shredded Fontina cheese

9 to 10 large shrimp (21-25 count), peeled, deveined, and sliced lengthwise

¼ medium red onion, peeled and thinly sliced

1 tablespoon thinly sliced fresh basil, for garnish

Kosher salt and freshly ground black pepper

1 One hour before baking, place a baking stone in the oven and preheat it to 500°F (450°F for gluten-free crusts).

2 Roll out 1 pizza round as thinly as possible and place it on a pizza peel sprinkled with flour. Leaving an outer lip all around the edge of the dough, cover the surface with half the garlic; season with salt and pepper.

3 Evenly spread half the pesto sauce on the dough. Top with the half each of the cheeses, shrimp, and onion.

4 Shake the peel lightly and slide the pizza onto the hot baking stone. Bake until browned, 6 to 7 minutes (10 to 14 minutes for gluten-free crusts).

5 Transfer the pizza to a firm surface and cut it into slices. Serve immediately, garnished with half the basil.

6 Repeat all the steps using the second dough round.

SCALLOP, BACON, SHALLOT, AND ASIAGO WITH CHIVES PIZZA

Scallops with bacon is a classic combination. Here, the scallops are paired with delicate shallots, nutty Asiago, and fresh chives to deliver incredible flavor. Make sure to ask your fishmonger for "dry" scallops, which are scallops that have not been treated with a preservative solution. "Wet" scallops hold on to too much water and don't sear well; they can also have off flavors and a rubbery texture.

1 tablespoon plus 2 teaspoons olive oil

½ pound dry sea scallops, patted dry

2 slices thick-cut bacon, cut into ¼-inch-long narrow strips ("lardons")

2 pizza rounds of your choice

All-purpose flour for sprinkling

½ teaspoon minced garlic

6 ounces Asiago cheese, thinly sliced

1 large shallot, peeled and thinly sliced

¼ cup coarsely grated Parmesan cheese

2 tablespoons chopped fresh chives, for garnish

Lemon wedges, for garnish

Kosher salt and freshly ground black pepper

1 One hour before baking, place a baking stone in the oven and preheat it to 500°F (450°F for gluten-free crusts).

2 In a medium skillet over high heat, heat 1 tablespoon of the oil until hot. Add the scallops in a single layer and sear them until golden brown, about 1 minute per side. Remove them immediately from the pan and set them aside. When the scallops are cool enough to handle, cut them into bite-size chunks.

3 Reduce the heat to medium-low. To the same pan, add the lardons and cook, stirring occasionally, until golden brown, 6 to 8 minutes. Transfer to a paper towel-lined plate to drain and set aside.

4 Roll out 1 pizza round as thinly as possible and place it on a pizza peel sprinkled with flour. Leaving an outer lip all around the edge of the dough, cover the surface with half the remaining oil and half the garlic; season with salt and pepper.

5 Evenly spread half the Asiago on the dough. Add half the reserved scallops and lardons. Top with half the shallot slices and half the Parmesan.

6 Shake the peel lightly and slide the pizza onto the hot baking stone. Bake until golden brown, 6 to 7 minutes (10 to 14 minutes for gluten-free crusts).

7 Transfer the pizza to a firm surface and cut it into slices. Serve immediately, garnished with half the chives, and lemon wedges.

8 Repeat all the steps (except steps 2 and 3) using the second dough round.

SMOKED SALMON FLATBREAD

We all know that smoked salmon goes well with cream cheese, but this garlic-and-herb Cheddar cheese flatbread with smoked salmon is a surprisingly delicious discovery. The smoked salmon is added just after the pizza comes out of the oven.

2 pizza rounds of your choice

All-purpose flour for sprinkling

2 teaspoons extra-virgin olive oil

8 ounces garlic-and-herb Cheddar cheese

½ red onion, peeled and thinly sliced

4 to 5 ounces smoked salmon, thinly sliced

1 tablespoon chopped fresh chives or scallion greens

1 teaspoon chopped fresh dill (optional)

Kosher salt and freshly ground black pepper

1 One hour before baking, place a baking stone in the oven and preheat it to 500°F (450°F for gluten-free crusts).

2 Roll out 1 pizza round as thinly as possible and place it on a pizza peel sprinkled with flour. Leaving an outer lip all around the edge of the dough, cover the surface with half the oil; season with salt and pepper.

3 Evenly distribute half each of the Cheddar and onion on the dough.

4 Shake the peel lightly and slide the pizza onto the hot baking stone. Bake until golden brown, 6 to 7 minutes (10 to 14 minutes for gluten-free crusts). As soon as the pizza comes out of the oven, drape it with half the salmon and garnish it with half the chives and dill, if using.

5 Transfer the pizza to a firm surface and cut it into slices. Serve immediately.

6 Repeat all the steps using the second dough round.

SHRIMP SCAMPI PIZZA

No one can really agree on the ingredient list for shrimp scampi, but garlic, parsley, and white wine are pretty standard (and tasty) bets. Don't use too much garlic sauce in step 4 or it could run off the pizza when you transfer it to the baking stone.

1 tablespoon plus 2 teaspoons extra-virgin olive oil

2 cloves garlic, minced

¼ teaspoon red pepper flakes

9 to 10 large shrimp (21-25 count), peeled, deveined, and sliced lengthwise

3 to 4 tablespoons dry white wine

2 tablespoons chopped fresh parsley, plus additional for garnish

2 pizza rounds of your choice

All-purpose flour for sprinkling

¼ cup coarsely grated Parmesan cheese

Lemon wedges, for serving

Kosher salt and freshly ground black pepper

1 One hour before baking, place a baking stone in the oven and preheat it to 500°F (450°F for gluten-free crusts).

2 In a large skillet over medium-high heat, heat 1 tablespoon of the oil. Add the garlic and pepper flakes and stir until fragrant, about 30 seconds. Add the shrimp in a single layer and sear them, 1 to 2 minutes per side. Remove the shrimp from the pan and set aside. Deglaze the pan with the wine, scraping up any brown bits. Reduce to a thick glaze then remove from the heat. Stir in the parsley and season with salt and pepper; set aside.

3 Roll out 1 pizza round as thinly as possible and place it on a pizza peel sprinkled with flour. Cover the surface with half the remaining oil and season with salt and pepper.

4 Leaving an outer lip all around the edge of the dough, spoon or brush some of the garlic glaze from the pan onto the dough. Top with half the shrimp and Parmesan.

5 Shake the peel lightly and slide the pizza onto the hot baking stone. Bake until golden brown, 6 to 7 minutes (10 to 14 minutes for gluten-free crusts).

6 Transfer the pizza to a firm surface and cut it into slices. Serve immediately, garnished with half the remaining parsley and lemon wedges.

7 Repeat all the steps (except step 2) using the second dough round.

ANCHOVY, SALSA VERDE, AND FRESH MOZZARELLA PIZZA

This pizza is full of bold flavors from the tangy, herby salsa verde to the salty, briny burst of anchovies. Keep the cheese nice and mild here—a fresh mozzarella is perfect.

2 pizza rounds of your choice

All-purpose flour for sprinkling

4 ounces fresh mozzarella cheese, torn into small pieces

6 to 8 anchovy fillets, rinsed if salt packed and patted dry

2 tablespoons Salsa Verde (see page 33)

Kosher salt and freshly ground black pepper

1 One hour before baking, place a baking stone in the oven and preheat it to 500°F (450°F for gluten-free crusts).

2 Roll out 1 pizza round as thinly as possible and place it on a pizza peel sprinkled with flour. Leaving an outer lip all around the edge of the dough, season the surface with salt and pepper.

3 Evenly spread half the mozzarella on the dough. Arrange half the anchovies in a pinwheel pattern on the pizza.

4 Shake the peel lightly and slide the pizza onto the hot baking stone. Bake until golden brown, 6 to 7 minutes (10 to 14 minutes for gluten-free crusts).

5 Transfer the pizza to a firm surface and cut it into slices. Serve immediately, drizzled with half the salsa verde.

6 Repeat all the steps using the second dough round.

7

SICILIAN-STYLE PIZZAS

Thick-crust, or Sicilian-style, pizzas are a world unto themselves. They are very distinctive, just as Sicily itself is different from the rest of Italy. These pizzas are beloved in America and are often synonymous with comfort—indeed, they're often known as "grandma" pizzas. The oil used in the pan makes for a deliciously crispy bottom crust, and the toppings are often bold.

CACIO E PEPE PIZZA

In Italian, *cacio e pepe* means "cheese and pepper," and it refers to the traditional Roman pasta dish of spaghetti with cracked black pepper and Pecorino Romano cheese. Here the same flavors are used to make a focaccia-like pizza that you can eat on its own or as an accompaniment to a meal. It's unbeatable for lunch with a green salad, or you might even want to top the pizza with a simple arugula salad. (Try the one from Pizza Bianco on page 58.)

1 Sicilian-Style Pizza Dough (see page 14)

¼ cup plus 2 tablespoons olive oil

½ teaspoon kosher salt

2 teaspoons coarsely cracked black pepper

⅓ cup Pecorino Romano cheese, coarsely grated

1 Preheat the oven to 500°F.

2 Coat a half sheet pan (see note on page 5) with ¼ cup of the oil. Transfer the dough to the pan and gently stretch it to fit the pan. If the dough springs back, let it rest for a few minutes before continuing. Using your fingertips, dimple the surface of the dough, then cover it with a sheet of plastic wrap and let it rise, 30 to 40 minutes.

3 Evenly spread the remaining oil, salt, and pepper on the dough, then top with the Pecorino Romano.

4 Bake the pizza until golden brown, about 20 minutes, then cut it into slices and serve.

GRANDMA PIE

Simple but utterly delicious, the classic grandma pie takes one of our main notions of pizza-making and literally flips it upside down. The cheese goes on first, before the sauce! While it's great as it is with just the delicious crust, sauce, and mozzarella, feel free to add the grated Parmesan or Pecorino Romano for some additional depth of flavor.

¼ cup extra-virgin olive oil

Sicilian-Style Pizza Dough (see page 14)

12 ounces mozzarella cheese, shredded

1½ cups Fresh Tomato Sauce (see page 20)

⅓ cup freshly grated Parmesan or Pecorino Romano cheese (optional)

1 Preheat the oven to 500°F.

2 Coat a half sheet pan (see note on page 5) with the oil. Transfer the dough to the pan and gently stretch it to fit the pan. If the dough springs back, let it rest for a few minutes before continuing. Using your fingertips, dimple the surface of the dough, then cover it with a sheet of plastic wrap and let it rise, 30 to 40 minutes.

3 Evenly sprinkle the mozzarella on the dough. Top with the sauce and the grated Parmesan, if using.

4 Bake the pizza until golden brown, about 20 minutes, then cut it into slices and serve.

ROASTED CHERRY TOMATO AND OREGANO PIZZA

A delicious variation on the Grandma Pie (see page 195), this pizza uses candy-sweet roasted cherry tomatoes, which ooze their juices all over the pizza.

¼ cup extra-virgin olive oil

Sicilian-Style Pizza Dough (see page 14)

12 ounces mozzarella cheese, shredded

1½ pounds Roasted Cherry Tomatoes (see page 42)

1 (2-ounce) tin anchovies (optional)

¼ cup freshly grated Parmesan or Pecorino Romano cheese

1 tablespoon chopped fresh oregano, or 1 teaspoon dried oregano

1 Preheat the oven to 500°F.

2 Coat a half sheet pan (see note on page 5) with the oil. Transfer the dough to the pan and gently stretch it to fit the pan. If the dough springs back, let it rest for a few minutes before continuing. Using your fingertips, dimple the surface of the dough, then cover it with a sheet of plastic wrap and let it rise, 30 to 40 minutes.

3 Evenly sprinkle the mozzarella on the dough. Top with the tomatoes and anchovies, if using. Sprinkle with the Parmesan and oregano.

4 Bake the pizza until golden brown, 20 to 25 minutes, then cut it into slices and serve.

HOT ITALIAN SAUSAGE, CARAMELIZED ONIONS, AND ROASTED RED PEPPER WITH DIJON MUSTARD AIOLI PIZZA

Full of bold flavors, this delicious pizza is spicy and complex. Don't fret if you don't have time to whip up the aioli—it's great even without it.

¼ cup extra-virgin olive oil

Sicilian-Style Pizza Dough (see page 14)

1½ cups Marinara Sauce (see page 16)

½ cup Caramelized Onions (see page 38)

½ cup sliced roasted red peppers from a jar

6 ounces (about ½ links) hot Italian sausage, cooked and sliced or crumbled

12 ounces mozzarella cheese, shredded

⅓ cup Mustard Aioli (see page 34)

1 Preheat the oven to 500°F.

2 Coat a half sheet pan (see note on page 5) with the oil. Transfer the dough to the pan and gently stretch it to fit the pan. If the dough springs back, let it rest for a few minutes before continuing. Using your fingertips, dimple the surface of the dough, then cover it with a sheet of plastic wrap and let it rise, 30 to 40 minutes.

3 Evenly spread the sauce on the dough. Top with the onions, peppers, sausage, and mozzarella.

4 Bake the pizza until golden brown, 20 to 25 minutes. Drizzle it lightly with the mustard aioli, then cut it into slices and serve.

PEPPERONI, SAUSAGE, AND FRESH TOMATO PIZZA

Diced tomato provides a fresh contrast to pepperoni and sausage, two perennial pizza favorites.

¼ cup extra-virgin olive oil

Sicilian-Style Pizza Dough (see page 14)

1½ cups Marinara Sauce (see page 16)

12 ounces mozzarella cheese, shredded

6 ounces (1 to 2 links) mild Italian sausage, cooked and sliced or crumbled

4 ounces pepperoni, thinly sliced

¼ cup freshly grated Parmesan or Pecorino Romano cheese

3 plum tomatoes, seeded, cored, and diced

1 Preheat the oven to 500°F.

2 Coat a half sheet pan (see note on page 5) with the oil. Transfer the dough to the pan and gently stretch it to fit the pan. If the dough springs back, let it rest for a few minutes before continuing. Using your fingertips, dimple the surface of the dough, then cover it with a sheet of plastic wrap and let it rise, 30 to 40 minutes.

3 Evenly spread the sauce on the dough. Top with the mozzarella, sausage, pepperoni, and Parmesan. Scatter with the diced tomatoes.

4 Bake the pizza until golden brown, 20 to 25 minutes, then cut it into slices and serve.

GREEK-STYLE PIZZA

Greek-style pizza is smothered in all of your favorite things—olives, onions, feta, oregano, and garlicky white bean hummus.

¼ cup extra-virgin olive oil

Sicilian-Style Pizza Dough (see page 14)

3 cloves garlic, chopped

½ cup feta cheese, crumbled

½ red onion, peeled and thinly sliced

¼ cup chopped oil-cured black olives (such as Kalamata)

1 tablespoon chopped fresh oregano

1¼ cups White Bean Hummus (see page 59)

1 Preheat the oven to 500°F.

2 Coat a half sheet pan (see note on page 5) with the oil. Transfer the dough to the pan and gently stretch it to fit the pan. If the dough springs back, let it rest for a few minutes before continuing. Using your fingertips, dimple the surface of the dough, then cover it with a sheet of plastic wrap and let it rise, 30 to 40 minutes.

3 Evenly distribute the garlic on the dough. Top with the feta, onion, and olives. Sprinkle with the oregano.

4 Bake the pizza until golden brown, 20 to 25 minutes. Dollop evenly with the hummus then cut it into slices and serve.

PEPPERONI AND JALAPEÑO PIZZA

If you like it hot, consider this pizza a good start. Pepperoni has its own heat, which is boosted here with jalapeño peppers, adding a delicious fresh note and crunch to the pizza. The pepper quantity below is not exact because heat level can vary from pepper to pepper. The optional pickled peppers offer yet another level of heat and a tangy contrast.

¼ cup extra-virgin olive oil

Sicilian-Style Pizza Dough (see page 14)

1½ cups Marinara Sauce (see page 16) or Fresh Tomato Sauce (see page 20)

12 ounces mozzarella cheese, shredded

⅓ cup freshly grated Parmesan or Pecorino Romano cheese

5 ounces pepperoni, thinly sliced

1 to 2 fresh jalapeño or serrano peppers, seeded and thinly sliced

Sliced pickled jalapeños or cherry peppers, for serving (optional)

1 Preheat the oven to 500°F.

2 Coat a half sheet pan (see note on page 5) with the oil. Transfer the dough to the pan and gently stretch it to fit the pan. If the dough springs back, let it rest for a few minutes before continuing. Using your fingertips, dimple the surface of the dough, then cover it with a sheet of plastic wrap and let it rise, 30 to 40 minutes.

3 Evenly spread the sauce on the dough, then top with the cheeses, pepperoni, and the fresh jalapeños.

4 Bake the pizza until golden brown, 20 to 25 minutes, then cut it into slices. Serve with pickled jalapeños, if desired.

ARTICHOKE, ASPARAGUS, BELL PEPPER, AND OLIVE PIZZA

Marinated artichokes, fresh asparagus, crunchy bell pepper, and cured olives make this pizza a study in delicious contrasts.

¼ cup extra-virgin olive oil

Sicilian-Style Pizza Dough (see page 14)

1½ cups Marinara Sauce (see page 16)

12 ounces mozzarella cheese, shredded

⅓ cup freshly grated Parmesan or Pecorino Romano cheese

1 (7.5-ounce) jar marinated artichoke hearts, drained

¼ pound asparagus stalks, blanched and cut into 1-inch lengths

½ red bell pepper, seeded and thinly sliced

½ green bell pepper, seeded and thinly sliced

2 small shallots, or ½ yellow onion, peeled and thinly sliced

⅓ cup sliced black olives

1 Preheat the oven to 500°F.

2 Coat a half sheet pan (see note on page 5) with the oil. Transfer the dough to the pan and gently stretch it to fit the pan. If the dough springs back, let it rest for a few minutes before continuing. Using your fingertips, dimple the surface of the dough, then cover it with a sheet of plastic wrap and let it rise, 30 to 40 minutes.

3 Evenly spread the sauce on the dough, then top with the cheeses and all the vegetables.

4 Bake the pizza until golden brown, 20 to 25 minutes, then cut it into slices and serve.

PISSALADIÈRE

You can't really call pissaladière "Sicilian style" because it's not; it's French—specifically, from Nice in the south of France. In fact, you probably can't even call it "pizza." It's a traditional pizza-like onion tart topped with black olives and anchovies. This version uses my regular pizza dough, though the original French dish is often made with puffed pastry. Traditionally, the anchovies are crisscrossed over the pizza with olives in between, but you can decorate it however you like. Pissaladière is tasty at any temperature and great with a nice green salad.

¼ cup extra-virgin olive oil

Sicilian-Style Pizza Dough (see page 14)

3 pounds Caramelized Onions (see page 38)

1 cup whole, pitted, oil-cured black olives (such as traditional Niçoise or Kalamata)

1 (2-ounce) tin anchovies

1 teaspoon chopped fresh thyme leaves

½ teaspoon chopped rosemary

1 Preheat the oven to 500°F.

2 Coat a half sheet pan (see note on page 5) with the oil. Transfer the dough to the pan and gently stretch it to fit the pan. If the dough springs back, let it rest for a few minutes before continuing. Using your fingertips, dimple the surface of the dough, then cover it with a sheet of plastic wrap and let it rise, 30 to 40 minutes.

3 Evenly distribute the onions on the dough. Top with the olives and the anchovies (in the crisscross pattern as described above, if desired) and sprinkle with the thyme and rosemary.

4 Bake the pizza until golden brown, 20 to 25 minutes, then cut it into slices and serve.

THE WORKS

It seems appropriate to end the book here, with The Works. The Works, also known as a "Supreme Pizza," has got a little bit of everything on it and is, in its own way, an American classic, though different variations have different combinations of toppings. Some people insist that it's not a pizza with the works if you don't have anchovies, so they're included here as an option in order to sidestep the controversy! If you don't have all of the items on the list, just leave out what you're missing or substitute another favorite topping.

¼ cup extra-virgin olive oil

Sicilian-Style Pizza Dough (see page 14)

1 cup Marinara Sauce (see page 16)

10 ounces mozzarella cheese, shredded

4 ounces pepperoni, thinly sliced

4 ounces (about 1 link) hot or sweet Italian sausage, cooked and crumbled

½ pound Italian Meatballs (see page 61), halved

1 green or red bell pepper, seeded and diced

4 ounces diced mushrooms, or ½ cup Sautéed Mushrooms (page 49)

⅓ cup sliced oil-cured black olives

½ red onion, peeled and thinly sliced

3 to 4 anchovy fillets, rinsed if salt packed and chopped (optional)

⅓ cup freshly grated Parmesan cheese

1 Preheat the oven to 500°F.

2 Coat a half sheet pan (see note on page 5) with the oil. Transfer the dough to the pan and gently stretch it to fit the pan. If the dough springs back, let it rest for a few minutes before continuing. Using your fingertips, dimple the surface of the dough, then cover it with a sheet of plastic wrap and let it rise, 30 to 40 minutes.

3 Evenly spread the sauce on the dough. Top with the mozzarella, pepperoni, sausage, meatballs, bell pepper, mushrooms, olives, onion, and anchovies, if using. Sprinkle with the Parmesan.

4 Bake the pizza until golden brown, 20 to 25 minutes, then cut it into slices and serve.

INDEX